A Daily Miracle

A Daily Miracle

Harold E. Dye

BROADMAN PRESS
Nashville, Tennessee

4250-26
ISBN: 0-8054-5026-2
Dewey Decimal Classification: 248.4
Subject Heading: CHRISTIAN LIFE//TIME
MANAGEMENT//MEDITATIONS
Library of Congress Catalog Card Number: 85-19453

Printed in the United States of America

Unless otherwise specified, Scripture quotations are from the King James Version of the Bible.

Scripture quotations marked (NASB) are from the *New American Standard Bible.* Copyright © The Lockman Foundation, 1960, 1962, 1963, 1968, 1971, 1972, 1973, 1975, 1977. Used by permission.

Scripture quotations marked (NEB) are from *The New English Bible.* Copyright © The Delegates of the Oxford University Press and the Syndics of the Cambridge University Press, 1961, 1970. Reprinted by permission.

Library of Congress Cataloging-in-Publication Data

Dye, Harold Eldon, 1907-
    A daily miracle.

    1. Time management—Religious aspects—Christianity.
I. Title.
BV4598.5.D94   1986   248.4   85-19453
ISBN 0-8054-5026-2

To Lila Belle, Joyce, Jeanne, and Leland
My grown-up kids who know how to love

Foreword

Time comes upon us, like Carl Sandburg's fog, on "little cat feet." It creeps upon us while we sleep, stalks us while we are awake. Unlike the fog, we cannot see it. The fog fills the eyes, the nostrils, the mouth, the ears. We can feel it; we can note the dampness crawling over our skin like a wooly worm, but we cannot frighten it away.

A new year comes in without fanfare. Nature does not sound off its advent with thunder echoing along the hills and valleys of our consciousness. Men may shoot off firecrackers and pistols, sound auto horns, and salute the newborn year with the noise of revelry, but time itself is silent. Time is dangerous to us, disquieting in its relentless march, terrifying in its finality. Time can take a big bite out of life—a bite that can kill even while we laugh.

Does that sound forbidding? Of course it does, but time has another face. January is named after the old Roman god, Janus. Janus had two faces, we recall. He could look in two directions at once—backward over tangled dreams and forward to the unknown. The forward-looking face of time is bright with promise. It promises reward for diligence, victory for patience, "joy unspeakable," and peace beyond understanding for those who live and walk and have their being in God, who holds all the future in His hands.

The purpose of this book is simple: that we might make time our servant and not our master in the constantly unwinding and raveling thread of life. It seeks the answer to the question: Where does time fit into the pattern of value priorities?

The book is written conversationally, much of it based on the author's personal experiences. After all, life has taught much to one who has lived with any degree of awareness over a span of eight decades.

Underlying its every statement is a shared faith in God, our Heavenly Father. It looks only one way—*up*—to the Creator who exploded the universe when time began and will dissolve the temporal heavens into the Eternal Heaven when time shall end.

My prayer is: May God bless this book to abundant usefulness in the life of the one who reads it.

Time Is

Too Slow for those who Wait,
Too Swift for those who Fear,
Too Long for those who
    Grieve,
Too Short for those who
    Rejoice;
    But for those who Love,
    Time is not.

—Henry Van Dyke

Contents

1
The Miracle Unfolds

The desert dawn splashed in my face, and I crawled out of my down-filled cocoon with drowsy reluctance. I was wide awake before I got the sleeping bag unzipped. I had the first dazzling glimpse of what I had come hoping to see. I watched God recreate the world.

Never before had anyone seen it in exactly the same way; no one else ever would. This was a miracle wrought specially for me. The sublime Artist was at work, and I stood barefooted before the divine glow as did Moses before the burning bush in a similar desert nearer to the dawn of time. In that far-off hour God recreated Moses. In these minutes before Him, He recreated me: He gave me the beginning of yet another day.

The reason this miracle was just for me is simple. No one else stood exactly where I stood in that precise moment of time! Therefore, no one else could have quite the same perspective. There was another breathtaking reason. God had never before used the same canvas or painted with the same strokes and never would again; both would be changed by the vanishing moment.

A man with clouded spiritual vision once commented to me, with a detectable sneer in his voice, "All desert mornings are just alike—monotonous." He must have seen only one. Sunrise on the desert, especially with the backdrop of giant mountains standing stark naked in a shower of variegated color, reflects an image as variable as a kaleidoscope.

Sometimes the sun rises quietly, unostentatiously. The first warning is a gradual lightening of the eastern sky above the cathedral spires of the rock-sheathed mountains. There is no color. The very next daybreak may be what the word implies—a veritable explosion of swirling colors with lacy cirrus clouds dancing in celestial ballet, their dainty technicolor gowns swishing almost with subtle sound.

The next morning the colors will be subdued. Long, pink fingers will push up the diaphanous curtain of the fading night and then reach down to place a golden crown on the mountain's shaggy head. Suddenly the glorious sun, like the chariot which the Polynesians so mystically describe, will mount the sky, throwing streamers of pastel-shaded light from its spinning wheels, splashing them on canyon walls and granite ramparts. They will gradually fall back and sink into the somnolent sand.

I watched such a splendored panorama for a rapt half hour. I could not see God's fingers at work, but I could see His beauty. I could not feel His breath, but I could feel His power. I knew better through that experience what Isaiah meant when he cried in awe, "I saw the Lord sitting on a throne, lofty and exalted, with the train of His robe filling the temple" (Isa. 6:1, NASB). My temple was not made with hands, and it stretched on forever.

I finally realized that the day was mine, to do with as I pleased and sent a prayer above the sunrise.

Return to that sunrise I had made my very own. You probably thought me egotistical in saying that God had created the miracle just for me. But I *am* someone special to God. So, too, are you. The breathtaking sunrise was merely the symbol of a new day—the miracle of time. You were not on the desert with me, and it was my loss, not yours; but you were *somewhere,* and covering that somewhere was the God of the *everywhere.*

Each of us will greet the new day in his or her own way; we cannot do otherwise. My precious little mother-in-law has said good-bye to earth and hello to heaven. But when she was ninety years old, she flew up to our home in San Jose, California, from her apartment in San Diego.

One morning I chided her for getting up so early. At five o'clock, she was already out of bed, puttering around in the kitchen, fixing coffee for herself, going out into the backyard, doing everything but what I thought she should be doing—sleeping until a decent hour.

"Why don't you stay in bed a little longer—at

least until daylight?" I demanded, as I sleepily groped my way into the living room.

"And miss the sunrise?" she asked. "I wouldn't do God that way . . ."

"You wouldn't do God what way?" I almost yelled.

"Refuse to receive His gift of the sunrise," she replied with a trace of excitement in her voice.

I opened my mouth—then closed it oh so slowly, my flippant rejoinder dead on my lips. I had started to say, "God will keep on making the sun to rise whether you watch it or not" or "God has made the sun come up beaucoup times, and He certainly would not care if you failed to see one of them" or "Just because He makes the sun come up, He doesn't expect you to jump out of bed to watch it." But those words stuck in my throat.

My mother-in-law traipsed out into the backyard, breathing deeply of the morning. I followed her with my own cup of coffee in my hand. The birds in our trees were singing their hearts out. Mother turned to me, her face radiant as that of an angel. "The birds make me think of what David said in one of the psalms. He said that he was going to wake up the morning with his song."

He did say it beautifully in Psalm 57:8: "I will awaken the dawn!" (NASB).

My frail "extra" mother, at ninety years of age, greeted the dawn of every new day with a song in her heart, thanking her Heavenly Father for the miracle He had wrought for her—someone special in His plan.

Now do you see what I meant? Another day, another miracle, just for you. There will never be another you.

My desert experience came as I was driving back from an engagement in Arizona. I did not provide the sunrise, of course, but I did plan for an extra day of solitude in the desert, alone with God and my meditations. This little book was conceived in a land called "barren" by those who do not know it.

I had driven my four-wheel-drive station wagon from a busy interstate highway some fifty miles over a winding, sandy road to a Jeep trail and had finally stopped at the end of that. I was then in a desert wilderness where no roads will ever be built and even Jeep tracks come to an end in order to protect the fragile ecosystem of the High Mojave. The altitude was above four thousand feet, and the time was April, the bright flowers were in full glory, and the birds were full of laughter.

I could have slept in the Jeep because I had removed the rear seat and had replaced it with an air mattress stretched back to the tailgate. I dismissed such creature comforts and slept under the stars. Have you ever slept under the desert stars? They are so close that you have to push them off of your chest; they seem to be hot enough to feel their heat. Compared to their beauty, the crown jewels of England are a handful of gravel.

I built a fire with wood that I had gathered back in Arizona and boiled coffee with water I had brought from home in a two-gallon thermos jug. My battered old coffee pot looks as though it has survived a dozen wars. I cooked ham and eggs, dumped them into a tin plate, and fixed toast in the pan I had freed.

It was now time to do what I had come to do. I strapped my canteen on my left hip and my .357 magnum revolver on my right. You see, the desert quickly reduces one to the basics of life, and this is good. The revolver was for old "Mojave Green." Mojave Green is not a bandit, but he is a murderer. He is a rattlesnake indigenous to this fierce land. In his viciousness he can make a three-foot-long Texas diamondback look like a skinned wooly worm. I had hand-loaded shotshell cartridges and stuffed them into the cylinder of the gun—just in case.

I wore heavy leather boots as protection against old Mojave Green if he saw me before I saw him. I also wore them for protection against the many kinds of cactus through which I would walk. This kind of place makes a fellow live up to the line in the Baptists' church covenant that promises to "walk circumspectly." If he doesn't, he may back into a jumping cholla cactus and get the seat of his pants, and the underlying epidermis, full of fishhook needles with no way to pull them out. I know.

I lifted my day pack to my shoulders. It contained a 35mm camera, telescopic and wide-angle lenses, as well as various filters, and a frugal lunch. I started out toward a distant hill. The first two miles I followed an arroyo (dry wash) because it was easier footing, then left it to cross over a rocky plateau.

To my right, a pile of huge rocks thrust upward from the sand to a height of about fifty feet. I carefully edged to the top of them and sat down on a ledge with a stone slab for a backrest. I pulled my binoculars from the pack, left them near my feet, and looked around. Backward over my left shoulder were the Providence Mountains, sentinels in the now blazing light of midmorning. To the northeast, the purplish range was in Nevada, some fifty miles away. Almost straight ahead was Death Valley, and beyond that something else. That "something else" brought my thoughts together.

On the eastern slopes of the Sierra Nevada grow the oldest living plants on the earth—the bristlecone pines. They were growing when Moses led the children of Israel out of Egypt toward the Promised Land. They could even have been growing when a bunch of crackpots tried to build a tower up to heaven, and God tangled them up in a confusion of unknown tongues to show them what imbeciles they were. God's practical joke was called the Tower of Babel.

A man wrote a book about the desert called *The Land that Time Forgot.* I never read it. Judging from the title, I don't think he knows what he was talking about. I have walked through those bristlecone pines, and I have thought: *If only they could talk, they could tell most of the recorded history of the world.*

Time walks the desert sands. A faint shadow stirred at the edge of a stone a few feet away from where I sat. As my eyes focused on it, I saw beady little eyes fastened on me. A wicked stinger tail looped over the creature's almost transparent body. It was a scorpion. I wanted to waste one of my snake loads on it but resisted the temptation. Scientists claim the lowly scorpion dates back a dreadfully long time.

Yes, the desert is ancient, ages piled upon ages in succession. It forces the mind toward philosophy and ultimately to the unanswerable, where faith must assume command, and theology becomes the final science.

My thoughts, as I sat on that rocky ledge looking at the vast sea of sand, led me back to the question raised by brains long stilled: *What is time?* That question has been asked by thinking men and women of every generation, and none has yet found the demonstrated answer. We have time for awhile, but all the while we are dumb before it.

Sixteen hundred years ago Augustine wrote these words: "What, then is time?" and added this comment, "If no one ever asks me, I know what it is. If I wish to explain it to him, I do not know." Augustine was both philosopher and theologian who wrote at length on the philosophical side of the question and then concluded that time is something which resides in the soul. His answer, to my own mind at least, is the most workable of all.

As far back as recorded thought, the greatest thinkers have posed this puzzling question. The Mesopotamians asked it in the land where the fake science of astrology was born. The Babylonians asked it in 1800 BC. In astrology, time resided in the stars and controlled every action of the human race, collectively and individually. Every event was timed by the decree of the stars and planets. The question was asked by Plato, Aristotle, Socrates, Pythagoras, and the Stoics, established by Zeno of Citium in the third century before Christ.

The ancients believed that time is circular—that is that time moves in cycles, and events of history will endlessly repeat themselves. That is why Plato and so many others believed in reincarnation. The belief in linear time (that time flies forward in a line as the arrow flies) is the heritage of Christianity. We know that: Christ was born on a certain date; He lived at a certain historical time embracing some thirty-three years upon the earth; He was crucified at a certain hour, dying physically upon a cross; on the third day He arose; and He will come back at the end of time. This is linear time. For centuries we have dated our calendars by it. Even atheists are forced to do so if they would live in any kind of world order.

Scientists will argue, but their arguments are really academic. We are amazed at this fact. In a day when so many men have walked on the moon and we have sent our space ships clear out of the solar system, if we ask any two physicists or astronomers whether time flows relentlessly on like a stream or flies straight as an arrow they will dispute each other by the hour. All the while, mindless time flows heedlessly past.

I asked a young astronomer from the Jet Propulson Laboratory at Pasadena the continuing question: "What is time?" This man had mapped the planet Venus from data sent back by one of our "fly-by" space birds.

His answer was both surprising and cocksure. "There is no such thing as time." When I said to him, "Prove it to me," he took me on a journey of 10,000 light years. As almost all of us know in these days of scientific enlightenment, a light year is the astronomer's way of measuring interstellar distances. That means it takes light, traveling at the speed of a tiny bit more than 186,000 miles per second, four and one-half years to reach the nearest star—Proxima Centauri. But here was a scientific "egghead" talking about 10,000 years—5,880,000,000,000 miles per year! That's even more figures than our national deficit.

"In the constellation Cygnus," explained the young man, "out near the limits of our galaxy, there is a binary star called Cygnus X-1. One star is about twenty-five times as large as the sun, and the other is a dark object of ten to fifteen solar masses. That is called a black hole. According to Einstein's special theory of relativity—which is absolutely true—time as we understand it is affected by both gravity and light. A black hole is a collapsed star, or even a collapsed galaxy such as our Milky Way, and the gravity which collapsed it is so strong that light cannot penetrate it. Time, at the perimeter of a black hole, is simply annihilated. It cannot exist. If time cannot exist there it, in fact, does not exist at all. Do you follow my reasoning?"

"How can I?" I answered, "when you have just annihilated my poor brain? I left it at the black hole."

I was thinking of all this as I sat on the desert rock and let time dribble through my mental fingers. I was a long way from camp, and the sun that started my day would soon sink behind the western hills. It was too late to continue on to my original objective —a flat-topped hill in the shimmering distance. It did not matter. I was on no assignment and had no boss. I had not snapped a shutter, but that did not matter either. I had enjoyed an unusual adventure of the mind and spirit. I had moved from earth to stars and to the God who made them.

I decided to take a longer trail back to the Jeep. The high plateau was studded with Joshua trees, and, although the walking would be harder, the extra scenery would be worth it.

A parting thought came to me as I lifted the day pack to my shoulders. If the wisest scientists could not explain time and if, as we believe, the unexplainable is a miracle, then time itself is the most amazing miracle of all, reexpressed every day of our lives upon the earth.

2
Time Is Life

The man from NASA was wrong. He may have been right scientifically—though astronomers are not all agreed on the existence of the so-called black holes in outer space. He may have been right philosophically. If the premise is true, the logical conclusions have to be.

But . . .

He was wrong practically—judging by the rules by which we are forced to live in this very real and unforgiving world. People do not live at the perimeter of a black hole at the cosmic edge of infinity. We shall never visit such a spatial mystery, no matter how fast we learn to fly. If Einstein's special theory of relativity is true (and it no doubt is), matter cannot be transported faster than the speed of light without its inevitable destruction into invisible particles. Humans would not only become timeless but also become nonexistent. Who among us wants to become a pinpoint of a billion subatomic neutrinos, whatever they might be? As Hamlet might say,

" 'Tis *not* a consummation devoutly to be wished." The idea expressed by my young acquaintance from the Jet Propulsion Laboratory was entertaining, titillating the mind, but I simply used it as a celestial hook upon which to hang some terrestrial—and vital—ideas.

The Reality of Time

Time cannot be put into a test tube by chemists and analyzed like a drop of water. It cannot be mathematically demonstrated by physicists with their computerized brains. It cannot be extinguished at a presumptive black hole where light collides with gravity and time thereby is killed. No philosophical hocus-pocus can make time disappear. We ordinary people, the *hoi polloi* if you please, know that time is real—we have to live by it, and that is *fact.*

Furthermore, life to you and me *is* a flowing stream of vanishing drops called seconds. According to how we feel, the stream may speed up or slow down; but it does go on as long as we do in our physical bodies. Let the intelligentsia try to balance on their noggins all they want to, but the rest of us will merely splash along the stream of life.

We cannot dam up the stream called *time* and say, authoritatively as Jesus said to the waves of Galilee, "Peace be still" (Mark 4:39). We cannot actually slow it down or abrogate its inexorable power. We cannot make it go backward no matter how plaintively or loudly we cry:

Backward, turn backward, O Time, in your flight,
Make me a child again just for tonight!

Time will refuse to heed our plea. Our hair will still grow gray or will fall away. Our vision will dim. Neither can we do what the science fiction writers suggest as parodied in the rhyme:

> There was a young lady named Bright,
> Whose speed was far faster than light;
> She set out one day/In a relative way,
> And returned home the previous night.

The only time we have is *now*. A young California man, the late Jim Croce, wrote a song immediately called a hit. The song was "Time in a Bottle." It is a haunting kind of song with a melody that lingers in the mind and heart, but it is the universal sentiment expressed which holds the soul. Croce sang about what he would do if he could bottle up time and use it as he desired. He would spend more of it with his loved ones—his pretty wife and baby. One by one he would drop the minutes into a jar. Then, when the jar was full, he would pour the minutes out as silver dollars of time, showering them upon those whom he loved.

Within a year of writing this lovely song, Jim Croce was killed in a plane crash. Had the young man, barely thirty, been able to do what he desired so wistfully, had he been able to drop the minutes into a bottle, the bottle would have been smashed in the same plane wreck.

We cannot put time in a bottle any more than we can bottle up the morning cloud and shield it from the burning sun or keep the sparkling dewdrops from drifting away from the faces of the violets. We cannot hoard the minutes, but we can use them wisely. They mark life.

Tick Tock, Tick Tock, Tick Tock

How many timepieces are there in your home? I counted those in and about our small house. A beautiful bracket clock graces the mantel of our fireplace. Its case is of hand-rubbed cherry, tastefully carved. The face is artistically etched copper with Roman numerals. The clock has Westminster chimes, four melodious notes on the quarter hour, eight on the half, twelve on the three quarters, and sixteen on the hour. At twelve o'clock it bongs sixteen times plus twelve—twenty-eight strikes in all. We can hear the clock with its tuneful reminders all over the house. The clock was a gift from my wife's Aunt Ruth with the admonition, "Don't waste time" —the motto by which she lived. A clock in my study stares over my shoulder now. It makes no sound but is one of those digital dingbats with the glowing numerals (like time itself) fading silently to the next. A clock with a beeping sound (another digital wonder) is in each of the three bedrooms. There is a clock in my workshop at the back of the lot.

Ina and I have wristwatches, as do most people in our country. Hers, since she is the industrious type, has to be wound every morning. I, being the lazy and forgetful type, have another digital "chronometer" on my own wrist. It is activated by a quartz crystal and runs on a tiny battery. It is much smarter than I am. It beeps on the hour, beeps an unwelcome summons when it is time to get up (if I ever need it), keeps tabs on the laps of a race (if I ever want to run one—or can); it is a stopwatch supposed to stop the seconds in mid-flight. It cost $29.95. My wife boils eggs to the dripping of sand in a vial (three seconds to the collective drips). It is one of the oldest kinds of timepieces known.

In the garden by the fish pond is my prized sundial—probably the oldest kind of timekeeper ever made except when God made the stars. My sundial keeps time to the accuracy of fifteen minutes, but I can't get it to adjust itself to daylight savings time. I haven't mentioned the timers that turn off the radio by our bed, the security lights, the washer, dryer, and even the furnace. Time lives in our home and never pays rent.

Your house is your castle, whether rented or owned. That is the law of the land. The one who enters your home without your permission can be arrested. Even law officers have to show a valid warrant issued by a judge before they can force their way through your door, or they, too, can be arrested and brought before the bar of justice. There is one intruder, however, that you cannot keep out. That intruder is above all human laws: time.

Your body, too, is inviolate according to law. Police officers will protect you from bodily harm if they can. The judge and jury are sworn to exact penalty from the one who willfully assaults you or takes your life except in self-defense.

But time is untouched by any code of civil behavior. You alone can partially control it. You alone can change a tyrant into a servant.

Time Has Another Name

Time's other name is most precious to us all. When I was in my early twenties, I wore two hats. I edited a small-town newspaper in Hagerman, New Mexico, in the richly productive Pecos Valley. I was also pastor of the First Baptist Church. The first was work; the second, fun. The second job was not only fun but also meshed well with the duties of the former. Twenty-three miles north of Hagerman is Roswell, the metropolis of the valley. Roswell supported two daily newspapers and was a bustling business center serving regional ranchers and farmers. It was a city of pleasant homes and thriving churches. A few miles west of Roswell on a high mesa, Dr. Robert Goddard, the "father of rocketry," was taking humanity's first step toward the moon.

Every Tuesday morning I drove to Roswell to solicit advertising for my little paper. One such morning I went into the upstairs office of an enterprising, young advertising director of the city's largest department store. His name was Tom Lawther. Tom, about my age, was a "go-getter" businessman. I don't know where he is today, but wherever he is, I venture to say he owns the store! I liked Tom mucho.

As I stepped into Tom's office that particular day, he jerked his thumb back over his shoulder and right in front of my eyes. There hung a neatly lettered sign:

TIME IS LIFE
DON'T MURDER ME

You see, even then, I talked too much. I have never forgotten Tom, and I never want to forget his sign.

Time Is Life

The theologian may quarrel with that statement and point out that Jesus said, "I am . . . the life" (John 14:6). That, of course, is blessedly true in the deepest sense. It is also true that the theologian may die while he is arguing this point. If so, time for him will have run out. This is not theological semantics; it is plain, unvarnished *truth.*

As far as I am personally concerned, when that "angel of death"—as Byron described him—taps me on my arthritic shoulder, and I find out what is going on, I will give him such a fight as will make Jacob's wrestling match at Peniel mere child's play. But eventually I'll go. You will when he lays his heavy hand upon you. We know this. It is the one fact we try to forget or ignore or even to outrun, but it will catch up with us. Time, therefore, gives life its urgency. They are inseparably bound together while we walk the paths of earth.

Time: The Attribute of Mortality

As long as we possess these mortal bodies, we live under time's determinism. God, alone, is untouched by time. He is the Great I AM—present tense. God is the Creator of time. Before there ever was a past, present, or future, Almighty God stood upon nothing and hurled time's golden chain down the darkened corridors of the ages, binding the three tenses to His will.

It is not too difficult for us to understand it was necessary for God to create time so He could speak into existence a universe which would *be* orderly and governed by law. Before time began, the earth was without form, void, chaotic. On the fourth day of creation, He created the sun, the Bible says, to rule by day and the moon to rule by night; He made the stars also. Normally the sun tells us when to work, the moon tells us when to sleep. The movement of the stars, moon, and planets regulate every mechanical clock on earth. It is so today when many of us are forced to believe that time, for the earth, is fast running out.

God the Eternal will remain. He was, He is, He ever shall be. The psalmist cried in ecstasy: "Before the mountains were brought forth, or ever thou hadst formed the earth and the world, even from everlasting to everlasting, thou art God" (Ps. 90:2). Isaiah chided the people: "Hast thou not known? hast thou not heard, that the everlasting God, the

Lord, the Creator of the ends of the earth, fainteth not, neither is weary?" (40:28).

The writer of Hebrews wrote of Jesus Christ—who is God—that He is the "same yesterday, and to-day, and for ever" (13:8).

This we believe. We also know that, as we are promised by Jesus Christ Himself in John 3:16, we who believe in Him have *everlasting* life. We are *eternal* souls. But, glorious as it is, all this knowledge is not enough. We are not yet in heaven. We are confined to the earth, with its pains, its sorrows, its sins, its disappointments, its failures, its frustrations, and many other spiritual enemies to our well-being.

That is why we treasure the words of David. Surrounded by his enemies, the warrior confessed to God with an outcry of faith: "My times are in thy hand" (Ps. 31:15). Blessed assurance! Our lives are bound up by time on the earth, but they are also bound up to God, the Everlasting, who never faints or grows weary; neither is His arm shortened that He cannot help.

Yes, Jesus did declare, "I am . . . the life," and hopefully you and I are glad to exult with David, "My times are in thy hand." Jesus also spoke concerning His mission on the earth: "I am come that they might have life, and that they might have it more abundantly" (John 10:10).

3
The Arrow of Time

Late afternoon shadows had begun to lengthen as the autumn day crept to its whispery close. The low, descending sun touched the treetops and sank toward the quiescent Mediterranean, setting the restless waves aflame and throwing wide bands of gold against the luminous sky like the banners of a retreating army.

Nature spoke with a muted voice, and the word was "peace" when there was little peace in the hearts of mankind. The Prince of peace had just been driven from the Temple in a shower of stones because He gave the truth to those who refused to hear it and offered hope to those who would not receive it.

A man in a ragged robe sat by the Temple gate, but his eyes did not see the sunset on the Mediterranean beyond the western horizon. They did not track the swooping swallows against the sky; his eyes saw nothing. They had never seen a day coming to life; neither the faces of loved ones going about their tasks. He could not even see the indifferent looks of those who refused him help.

He could only stare vacantly at nothing as he had done ever since, as a babe, he had first opened his eyes on darkness. Had it not been the sabbath day, and therefore illegal to beg for alms, the man would have sat stretching out pitiful hands and whimpering, "Gain merit by me! Gain merit by me!" As it was he simply sat, his sightless eyes rolling in nettlesome night and his heart like lead beneath his ribs.

Jesus stopped in His hurried retreat from the Temple. His own eyes, which saw everything, had seen the helpless, hopeless beggar who asked nothing with his lips but simply let his affliction cry out for any answer to his needs. That has always been enough for the blessed heart of Jesus.

The disciples followed the Master's eyes. Where Jesus saw a person, they merely saw a problem. Besides, the hour was late, and danger dogged their heels.

"Who did sin, . . . that he was born blind? (see John 9:1-38). The question was empty, barren as the sand beneath their sandals. What difference did the why make? The man was blind. That, alone, was what should have mattered to them.

The dust of two thousand years has blown across this scene near the Temple gate, but the picture is still with us. While people suffer, we trot out tired philosophies and sociological bandages. Suffering has never been driven away by explanation: not then, not now.

Jesus did give a clear explanation of His own motivation. "I must work the works of him that sent me, while it is day: the night cometh, when no man can work" (v. 4).

That was the last autumn our Lord would ever see while He wore the human flesh. It would have been His last day on the earth if the Jews of the Temple had had their way. His body would have right then lain broken by the murderous rocks hurled by those whom He had come to save. The fact that his hour was "not yet come" did not obviate the crime perpetrated in the hearts of His enemies. The earthly life of our Lord was rapidly drawing to a close; His one brief day was far spent. He would soon see His last evening as it touched the hill Golgotha.

It is utterly presumptuous to put thoughts into the mind of Jesus, but we cannot help but wonder. Was He thinking of Himself? How could He have kept from it? Most of all, though, He was thinking of the poor man's need, both physical and spiritual. The Greek wording of John 9:4 is: We must work the works of him who sent me. That makes each of us a partner with Christ in doing good. We can neither cure physical nor spiritual blindness, but we can point people to the One who can. We can accept this beggar's blindness as symbolic of any great need that anyone has. The caution is the simple word *now*.

Since anyone likely to read this book will already

know the beautiful story of the healing of the blind man, it is unnecessary to recount it here. (If one does not know it, the event is described in the ninth chapter of the Book of John.) Attention is simply called here to the urgency of our doing what we can do *while we still can.*

The Night Cometh

At the age of twenty-six, Sir Walter Scott had the words *Erchetai Nux* inscribed on the sundial in his garden. His bride of a few days asked the meaning of the Greek words, and the author said, "The night cometh." She shuddered and asked that he have the dismal words removed. Her husband refused with the gentle explanation, "I need to remind myself that when I walk in this peaceful, restful place, I must not tarry too long. I have much work to do." Another great English literary genius, Dr. Samuel Johnson, had the same words inscribed on the face of his watch for the same reason. Thomas Carlyle wrote them in his first book, *Cometh Night,* and Robert Murray McCheyne signed his delightful letters with the reminder, "Cometh Night."

A poet wrote:

> We have not time
> To play, to dream, to drift—
> We have lots of hard work to do
> And loads to lift.

Frost looked into his own frailty; but in doing so, he touched the frailty of us all. Our feet lead us to such pleasant places that we are tempted to build tabernacles of the spirit while life, itself, passes us by, the daylight fades, and the night closes in.

The other night I awoke at midnight and was still awake at dawn. Since I am seventy-eight years of age, it suddenly dawned upon me that I could never do the things I had dreamed of through my lifetime. My goals had always exceeded my grasp. That within itself is not bad. What tormented me that sleepless, painful time was: I would leave undone things that I could have accomplished with so little effort—but I did not.

For instance I have in one desk drawer at least one hundred unanswered letters. Most of them date back several years. I remembered that one week alone I had received letters from three men in their nineties. The letters came as a result of some Sunday School lessons I had written for senior adults. The letters are heartwarming, and I felt uplifted when I read them. But I was busy. I felt I had either the choice of carrying my excessively heavy load of writing assignments or answering unsolicited mail. So I put off answering the letters, and every one of my well-meaning friends felt rebuffed.

You are probably thinking: *Why didn't he just get up out of bed, where he was sleepless anyway, and answer those letters?* I started to do exactly that with regard to the three ninety-year-old men. Then the cold chills crawled down my spine. It was likely that after this long a time, all three of them were dead. This reminded me of my wife's heart-tearing experience a

few years ago. She was the teacher of a women's
Sunday School class, and one of the women was
absent for three consecutive Sundays. Ina wrote her
a letter expressing disappointment at her absence
from class. The letter came back with a curt little
note from the woman's daughter: "Mother died a
week ago." My wife burst into uncontrollable tears
and will carry the scars of that tragedy as long as she
lives. My own psyche bears similar scars.

J. Winston Pearce and his wife, Winnie, are popular speakers at various meetings all over America.
These latter days they are especially welcomed at
senior adult conferences not simply because of their
wisdom and knowledge but because of their genuine love which they do not try to conceal. Both are
successful authors. Winston has a book on letter
writing that is a "must" for everyone who wants to
be of lasting service to others. It is called: *Say It With
Letters* (Broadman Press, 1981). I was most im-
pressed by the book not so much by what the author
said—though it was helpful—but by my personal
knowledge that the author practices what he
preaches. He writes simple, short notes in his own
handwriting (when I try that it looks like hen
scratching in the dirt).

Here is an example of words that lifted my spirit.
I had written a little book about a Mexican boy and
his aunt living on a ranch in Arizona. This is what
Winston wrote about it in a note to me: "You have
loved them into existence." I shall always treasure
that letter because my friend captured my own heart

with his soulful words—six of them. Of course, it was a high compliment from such a master author, but it was more—infinitely more. It was a meeting of our own hearts. I doubt that it took my delightful friend more than a minute or two to write that note, and I received it nearly twenty years ago.

As my sensitive little wife found out the hard way, dead persons do not read letters. Neither, I might add, do they write them. The day—whatever our age—is far spent.

My night of torment carried many other heartaches. I thought of Ben Truman—and several others. Let me tell you about Ben. He was a half-breed Choctaw Indian. He and his wife attended a little halftime church in New Mexico which I pastored when I was in my early twenties. Ben liked me, and I liked him—immensely. He laid one taboo on me however. I was not to try to talk to him about his soul's salvation. A loud-mouthed sort of fellow, he had threatened bodily harm to anyone who had the temerity to approach him during the invitation at the end of the service. He would come to church if we all obeyed his rules.

After I had been gone for years, my wife and I went back for revival services, and we stayed in Ben's home. They came to the services but always sat on the back pew. I could feel Ben's hypnotic eyes upon me while I preached.

The meeting was drawing to a close. I gave the invitation as urgently as I could and prayed that Ben would accept it. Suddenly I froze. Ina had slipped quietly back to Ben's side, had put her arm on his shoulder, and was talking earnestly with him. He shook his head and was the first through the door when the meeting was over. As we drove the five miles out to the Truman farm, Ina said, "I know that we are in trouble, but I couldn't help it. I just had to speak to him. Now, I am afraid." "So am I," I admitted, "but I'll tell you what. When we walk in, you stay right behind me, and Ben will have to work me over before he can get ugly with you."

We entered the living room without knocking. Ben sat in his overstuffed chair, face buried in a newspaper. His wife sat nervously twisting her handkerchief in her hands. We intended to slip right on by into our room and to bed, but it was not to be so easy. Ben got up. He was big, broad shouldered, narrow hipped. He could have taken me apart without half trying. He started toward us, and I spread my feet and prepared to defend Ina and myself. I did not feel heroic.

"Come out from behind that little squirt!" Ben roared at Ina. She stepped out and looked up into his face unflinchingly.

"You were scared to death of me, weren't you, girl?" Ben said. "Old Ben would never hurt you. Don't you know that?"

"I had to do what I did, Ben," Ina answered, "because I love you and want to see you saved."

The big Indian caught her by the shoulders and looked deep into her eyes. "Thank you," he replied simply. "Maybe someday . . ." His voice trailed off, but he never did.

There came a day when I drove 250 miles from my home and over two mountain ranges to bring the message at my friend's funeral. It was his dying request. The services were held in the same church auditorium where Ina and I, using different methods, had tried to reach Ben for the Lord.

Any God-called pastor knows my feeling as I lay awake that dreadful night thinking about Ben and others over whose names I would have to write, "Almost persuaded." You perhaps have known it, too, in your life. The ultimate question is not, Did I succeed? Rather it is, Did I try my best?

When the night comes to us, we cannot cry as Christ did from the darkness of the cross—*tetelestai* —done! He alone could say: "It is finished" (John 19:30). We shall die leaving many things undone. They carried Raphael into his studio for a last look at his unfinished masterpiece *The Transfiguration*, and he cried, "Alas, it will never be completed." Catherine the Great, the empress of Russia, moaned when darkness fell on so many of her unfinished projects: "I am an accumulation of broken ends." No, we cannot do it all, but we can be faithful in our service. We are busy people. We do not twiddle our thumbs in idleness. We do need to ask ourselves, though, Am I busy about the most important matters? Night comes. While we misuse time, does opportunity slip away?

Gracious Partnership

"We must work," said Jesus. Partners with God! What an honor!

My father-in-law, dead for many years, shared this story with me. He once drove a Stanley Steamer stage for the Santa Fe Railway around the famed Tonto Rim of the fabulous Grand Canyon. He stopped at various scenic points to let the passengers view the beauties of this natural wonder. One day there were only two riders, a young fellow and his girl friend. They got out at Yavapai Point and walked over to the edge. The girl gave a quick glance; then, with compact in hand, began to powder her nose. She dismissed the geologic masterpiece with the words, "Isn't it cute?"

My father-in-law-to-be remarked, "I wanted to push her into it." The next day his passenger list had one lone man. My pa-in-law drove him to the same scenic point. The man walked over to the edge and stood in rapt and continuing admiration. He watched the play of colors on the pinnacles and steeples of a mighty temple of the Lord. My father-in-law finally had to tap him on the shoulder to make him leave.

On the way back to the El Tovar Hotel, my father-in-law told the man of the experience from the day before and the flippant reaction of the cosmetic queen, and said, "I'm going to quit this job. I am tired of carrying thoughtless dudes around who can't even see what they came to see."

The man's quiet answer was, "Only God could have made the Grand Canyon. Why don't you consider yourself His partner in showing His handiwork?" When he left the stage, he gave my father-in-law a card on which was engraved the name "Arthur Brisbane." Arthur Brisbane became the highest-paid columnist of his time. What did he write about? The glorification of common labor.

Most of us live our lives without public acclaim or even public attention. What difference does it make? We live to hear One say, when this life on earth is over, "Well done" (Luke 19:17). It is enough.

Jesus caused a blind man to see. We can help those who are spiritually blind to see Him. To that task we dedicate ourselves until night comes.

The great Britist astronomer, Sir Arthur Eddington, born more than one hundred years ago, coined a descriptive phrase favored by today's scientific writers delving into the mystery of time. Eddington referred to "the arrow of time." I like that for reasons other than those expressed by the writers.

I own a powerful bow. I can knock an arrow, pull it back until the feather almost touches my ear, and loose the arrow into the air. If I aim upward on an arc, the arrow will fly out of sight. It will leave no track to show where it has been. It will spend itself noiselessly, and, no matter how far it goes, it will finally drop back to the earth. There are both a beginning and a end to the arrow's flight. That, too, is like time.

There is another thought. The arrow is an archer's weapon. The word translated *sin* in the Bible is also an archer's word. It literally means "to miss the mark." We easily identify such terms as adultery, murder, lying, stealing, and cursing as relating to sin. We can understand sins of the flesh. There is another sin which we sometimes ignore. James said, "Therefore to him that knoweth to do good, and doeth it not, to him it is sin" (Jas. 4:17). This, too, is missing the mark. Let the arrow of time fly true, on target. Being on target for Jesus is marvelous.

4
Nailing Down Time

How often do you hear someone ask, "Whatever happened to the time?" If you are of middle age or older, you hear it almost every time you have a lengthy conversation with one of your peers. You ask it of your own mind in a hopeless sort of way. When the thought is voiced, it is not with curiosity but with dismal resignation. The older we get, the more we realize the fleeting nature of the very essence of life.

There was a period when time crawled for you. When you were a kid, the longest whole week in the year began December 20 and ended at five the morning of December 25. What were the names of Santa's reindeer? I can only remember Dancer and Prancer. Those seemed to be funny names for a couple of snails. Snails can't fly. They can't even walk. They just kind of ooze along, leaving a slimy, silver-looking trail behind. Of course, modern kids don't believe in Santa. They simply pretend to. They're not dummies. Remember, they sat on Santa's lap at Macy's, I. Magnins, Emporium-Capwells, and Woolworth's. They may even put two bits in the Salvation Army kettle to sit on the old fellow's lap in front of the post office. They do buy the idea, though, that old Santa, no matter who he is, travels s-s-l-l-o-o-w-w-w.

But how about you? Before you can remove the cost of that silly-looking stuffed doll off your credit card, it is time for the old fat guy in the red britches to slide down the old gas pipe again. Time flies for you now, but it was not always that way.

The longest year of my entire life was the eleventh. I wanted to become a Boy Scout. There was nothing—absolutely nothing—in the whole, wide world I wanted more. The Boy Scout movement was just my age. In the year I was born, Sir Robert Baden-Powell, a fifty-year-old retired British officer and part-time writer, took twenty-five boys on a camping trip to Brownsea Island, off the coast of England. He had found, as a general in Africa, that the men sent to him for army service were too soft. He decided to build real men by teaching young boys self-reliance and encouraging them in physical hardness. They learned some of both on that memorable camping trip. They learned to swim, took long hikes, practiced tying knots, built shelters, ate a few bugs in the interest of survival, and learned how to cook simple foods.

Among other accomplishments, they learned how to cook a "hunter's twist." Do you know what that is? If you don't, you are a gourmet illiterate. You are also gastronomically deprived. Hunter's twist is a kind of bread made by twisting a spiral of dough around a green stick and cooking it over hot coals. I can still cook one that would make the head chef of the Waldorf-Astoria green with envy.

Anyway, when the little expedition returned to England, Baden-Powell started his famed program for boys. The movement soon spread to other countries. The boys wore natty uniforms, khaki shirts with rank patches, khaki shorts, and even khaki socks. Their army-type hats had brass achievement badges: Tenderfoot, Second Class, and First Class. These kids were sharp!

I simply had to become a Boy Scout. The trouble was: I was just eleven, and the beginning Scout age was twelve. In order to ease the pain of time waiting, I became what was known as a Junior Scout—later Cub Scout. The Cub Scouts were organized by dens instead of troops. They had "den mothers." In a kind of reverse discrimination, a man could not be a den mother. That made the whole deal "sissified" as far as I was concerned. I hated the idea, but I stuck it out—one whole year. It was the longest year of my life. Then I became a Boy Scout and was connected with Scouting well into my adult life.

Bored? But I am trying to illustrate how time flies —for us all.

My wife was nineteen, and I was twenty when we were married. If we live until next year we shall have been married sixty years. I had to have my father's written permission to commit the act of matrimony since I was under legal age in New Mexico. That was a galling experience to me.

I was ordained to the gospel ministry at nineteen and became pastor of a small church during college days when I was twenty. At twenty-seven, I was called as pastor of First Baptist Church in Las Cruces, New Mexico. That was the home of State A. and M. College (now New Mexico State University). I was called "kid preacher" by townspeople— among other titles. Today, of course, I could have remedied part of that by growing a beard, and then I would have looked like an old goat, but in those days, I would have been laughed out of town.

I couldn't wait to "mature." Then the very minute they stopped calling me a kid preacher, I was too old! Pulpit committees seemed to be interested in "baby faces." Now that I am nearing eighty, I am an "enemy of the young" because some claim they are having to support me through their own payments to Social Security and Medicare. I am also considered "senile" by some of them—probably with a bit of justification.

Have I struck a responsive chord in you—whatever your age? As long as you live, you will be plagued by the question, What happened to time? Where did it go so fast? We scarcely experience a single moment before it is gone, never to return.

There is, though, infinite worth in a finite moment in time. We once had a couple in our church who celebrated their diamond wedding anniversary —seventy-five years together. The man was ninety-four, and his bride was ninety-two. When he was sixteen, he whispered to a fourteen-year-old girl, "I love you." It required him two seconds to say it. Seventy-five years later before our congregation, he repeated that tender declaration to his diminutive, gray-haired wife. His two-second "I love you" had stretched into seventy-five happy years! Not even that is the end of the story. Paul listed love as the greatest of the triumvirate of imperishables in the thirteenth chapter of First Corinthians. Time's whirling seconds will vanish, but love will last through all eternity.

Nailing Down Time

I cannot shake the feeling of hypocrisy as I write this chapter. No one is more adept at wasting time than I. In the first place, I have a "grasshopper" mind. It jumps from one thought to another without digesting either. (I just glanced out through my study window. The grass needs mowing. When did I mow it last? Why does it have to grow so fast? I suppose I'll mow it Saturday, but what if it rains Saturday?) Now, where was I? Oh, yes, I was preparing to tell you how to conserve time. Paul warned against my kind of mind. "This one thing I do," he said to the Philippians (3:13). He said more, but hold on to this: We need to set our goals in life, and we must concentrate those purposes. That means staying with a task until it is accomplished. The mind is a mighty ally, but it can also be a ruthless enemy.

Here is another failure of mine. (I present myself in the belief that we can learn good lessons from bad examples.) Through the years I have impoverished myself by using not only thought processes but also working methods as organized as bowls of mulligan stew. For instance, some thirty-two years ago I built the house in which we are now living. I built it from the foundation to the roof with my own blistered hands. I spent more time hunting my hammer than I did driving nails. A well-planned and catalogued filing cabinet with clippings of interest gathered through the decades would be invaluable to me now that a part of my brain has begun to petrify—and putrify. What is more, I could have used such a system to tremendous advantage through the flying years.

Here is another example of my idiocy. The top right-hand drawer of my desk contains my address filing system. When I get a letter with a printed return address and think I might need it sometime, I tear that corner off the envelope and drop it into the drawer. Then all I have to do is dig out all of those slips and look through them, and—*voilá*—there it is—with only one hour lost! My workshop is so cluttered I may fall over a pile of wood sometime and cut off my head with the ten-inch table saw. I won't tell you about the garage where I can't find room for the car because . . .

There *is* another side. My neighbor Art shames me. His yard is manicured. He mows his grass one way, then turns around and mows it crosswise. He trims his hedge the way a hairstylist teases hair. By hand he even picks up stray leaves from the ash tree in the center of the yard, so he won't disturb the grass. His backyard with its immaculate swimming pool looks like a landscaped park. I could eat ice cream off of his work bench with a spoon and never taste any sawdust.

My neighbor is a slave to his methodization. (As you can see, I am no "methodist.") The only reading he ever does is the morning newspaper, and he skips the editorial and op-ed pages in that. I like him, but I would like him better if he didn't come out to help me in everything I try to do.

He tells me (taking my wrench out of my hand to demonstrate) how to change the spark plugs on my car. He tells me (taking the shears out of my hand) how to prune the rose bushes. He is even more of a slave than I am. My neighbor pigeonholes his every thought in a neat row of labeled mental boxes. He never thinks except in a straight line from point *A* to point *B*.

Martha, in the home in Bethany, was encumbered by the mechanics of putting the salad on the left (if that was where it is supposed to go) when Jesus came to visit. That showed both industry and thoughtfulness, but Mary chose an approach more pleasing to her Lord: she sat at his feet while He broke the bread of life with her.

A victorious life must consist of a balanced system of choosing priorities: the safeguarding of time for one purpose—to put it to its best use. In the greatest

discourse on time ever written, the writer of Ec-
clesiastes mused, "To every thing there is a season, and a time to every purpose under the heaven"
(3:1).

Making Time Count

Jesus came out of eternity where there is no time
to earth where He spent three short years of earth's
seasons. He came with a single purpose: to seek and
to save the lost (see Luke 19:10). Never for a moment did He lose sight of that objective. Those
short years He went about doing good. That
thought thrusts a challenge toward us. Are we, who
call His name in faith, going to be content with
simply "going around"? Three short years—yet He
made time for beggars even while He set up a king-
dom that would outlive all the earthly kingdoms for
all time to come. Inhumanly busy as He was, Jesus
did not think it robbery to spend time in prayer. He
never once sacrificed spirituality to expediency. He
never got His priorities mixed or lost in the fog.
Three short years and He went back to heaven, leaving His purpose with us, confident that we would
not fail Him. This is our urgency; this is our ultimate
reason for living.

The proper management of our time is impera-
tive, but it must not be merely mechanical—a
straightjacket, limiting human interchange. If making a dollar keeps us from the time it takes to make
a friend, we had better skip a meal or two. After all,
a dollar won't buy any pleasure in heaven.

Time for God

For the last twenty-two years of my pastoral ministry, I served Baptist Temple in San Jose, California. The greater metropolitan area of San Jose consists of more than one million people. It is really a part of a megalopolis stretching all the way to San Francisco on the north—fifty miles of adjoining houses and businesses. I averaged some two thousand miles per month driving traffic-infested streets. One day, as I sat fuming ninety seconds at a traffic light waiting for the red light to change to green, I thought, *When I die, how much of my life will have been spent waiting for the lights to change?* Ten lights per day (probably my average) would add up to 60 hours per year, 1,320 in 22 years or 165 working days. Even if I halved that, it would still be 82 working days waiting for the light to change! By that time the driver behind me was honking his horn like mad.

Then I thought of L. A. Grantham and his wife. Grantham was an insurance man. He could quote and apply more Scriptures than any layman I ever knew. I once asked him how he learned so many. He and his wife had then moved to Phoenix which was growing rapidly and had become afflicted with stoplights. Grantham responded, "I got so mad waiting, killing time while those lights changed, that I decided I would just put that time to constructive use." He started every day by attaching a piece of paper to the sun visor over the windshield. On that little piece of paper, he had written a Scripture verse. It took about two stoplights for him to memorize the verse and lodge it in his mind and heart. Can you think of a better way to treat frustration than to make it your servant in life enrichment?

Now, let me tell you about Mrs. Grantham. She was given a women's class to teach. Before long, it outgrew its meeting room. Then it outgrew another. Finally the class had to meet in the church auditorium because of its popular teacher.

Mrs. Grantham was the mother of two teenage boys. She stayed busy washing clothes and feeding the boys and her husband nourishing meals. Besides this, she kept a spotlessly clean house.

One day my wife and I visited this Sunday school teacher. She stopped washing dishes long enough to visit with us. After a while I went into the kitchen for a drink of water. Then I found out one thing that made this consecrated women such a splendid teacher. Her teacher's quarterly was pinned, open, to the curtain over her sink, so she could study her lesson while she did the dishes. Is it any wonder that overworked housewife brought eternal blessings to those whom she taught?

Life Like a Vapor

James asked the question I am threading through these pages: "For what is your life? It is even a vapour, that appeareth for a little time, and then vanisheth away" (Jas. 4:14). He was speaking of the brevity of life, of course. But there is more to vapor than elusiveness. Steam is vapor. It does not last long and, turned loose, disappears into the air with scarcely a trace. Properly harnessed and timed, though, steam can move a mighty locomotive, pulling a heavy string of one hundred freight cars. Our lives will be short; but harnessed to the Holy Spirit, they can be powerful.

As the psalmist besought the Lord in the ancient prayer, we too pray, "So teach us to number our days, that we may apply our hearts unto wisdom" (90:12).

5
To Each His Own Time

Are you ready for the sad tale of Burro Schmidt? You never heard of him? Read on; his story carries a lesson for us all. The respected *Bakersfield Californi-an* in a feature article last week reported that 200 to 300 visitors will brave four-wheel-drive rides Easter Sunday far into the Mojave Desert to see a hole in a mountain. That hole is all that is left of Burro Schmidt's life. He buried thirty-eight years in it.

I wrote the story of the old desert rat some twenty-five years ago. Few people knew about him then. Here is how I wrote it. I called the piece:

The Glory Hole

The bright ribbon of asphalt stretched through the parched, barren, rocky hills like a lazy, silver snake. The wheels of our Jeep hummed gently, and the ugly snout seemed to be gobbling up the snake.

It was early morning, and the sun had burst over the fierce Panamints to the east where storied Death Valley lay bathed in shimmering waves of eternal heat. As the sun soared higher, it tinted the granite walls of the rugged desert mountains, softening them and leaving them awash with a supernal glow.

I was entranced by the strange, mystic beauty of this wild land over which hung an untranslatable feeling of death. But all was not dead. Here and there a carpet of golden California poppies folded back from the base of a hill, or a cluster of lupines looked like pools of water splashing against a rocky shore.

Suddenly a voice spoke in my ear. "See that there round knob of a hill over on your left? That's where old Burro Schmidt dug his glory hole."

"What?" I asked, brought back from my reverie with a jar. "Just who was Burro Schmidt, and why did he dig a hole? I seem to be a little ignorant."

"You mean you never heard of Burro Schmidt?" came the astonished question from Bill Stamps, amateur prospector and my companion on the trip.

There was a note of anguish in his voice, and I felt slightly like an unfeeling clod in my failure properly to inform myself of the life and activities of one Burro Schmidt. I contritely proposed that Bill alleviate my ignorance, as the Mexican says, *muy pronto.*

Now here comes the story of the incredible Burro Schmidt. Read it and wonder.

High in the El Paso Range in the upper reaches of Mesquite and Last Chance Canyons in the wild desert country of California, a man staggered out into the sunshine and shook the powdery dust from his hair and eyebrows. He had come half a mile, but it had taken him thirty-eight years—just two less than the Israelites wandered in the wilderness. At long last "Burro" Schmidt had reached his promised land—the other side of a bleak hill. For thirty-eight years he had been nothing but a human mole, burrowing, burrowing, digging with clawlike hands wrapped around a slick pick or shovel handle while he forced his way through a mountain of rock. Behind him lay a tunnel, two thousand feet long, in which lay buried half his life.

William H. Schmidt was born in Woonsocket, Rhode Island, January 30, 1871. He had three sisters and brothers who never reached the age of thirty years. All died of consumpton. In order to escape the ravages of the dread disease, the young man came to the desert and joined the prospectors who were working the area around Randsburg, which was yielding considerable gold and other metals. In 1906, the year of the San Francisco earthquake and fire, Schmidt started digging an exploratory drift abandoned by a mining syndicate from Bakersfield. About fifty feet in, he struck the only commercial possibilities of the entire half mile of hole—gold, silver, copper, iron, and molybdenum. In order to simplify the problem of getting the ore to a smelter and avoid building several miles of railroad, Schmidt decided to drive a tunnel through the heart of Copper Mountain. He did it—in thirty-eight years!

His only light came from the guttering candles which he bought at three for five cents.

Using hand tools, he dug away at the vitals of the mountain. His blasting was done with 40 percent dynamite. He cut his fuses short—endangering his life with every blast—so that his supplies would last longer. He loaded the tunnel muck, more than twenty-six hundred cubic yards, on a single ore car which he pushed by hand to the dump.

All of this time the man now called Burro lived in a shack a short distance from the tunnel mouth. He lived on flapjacks and beans with sometimes the luxury of "fish chowder" of boiled onions, rice, and sardines. He cooked more than twenty-five thousand meals on the stove in that cabin with no one to share them but a lizard now and then. His only other companions were a couple of burros which gave him their name. His clothing was patched-up discards of other miners.

Finally he came out of the hole. He was eighty-two years of age. He could not stand up straight because his back was permanently bent from the work in constricted places.

Behind him, in the dust of the hole, were the ground out elements of a man's life—his opportunities for love, human companionships, material comforts, and, what is most important, for services to the God who created him.

Why? At the prevailing wages of his day, the labor of this man was worth forty-four thousand dollars during the years he spent in the barren hole. When he finally finished the tunnel, he took out twenty tons of ore that assayed sixty dollars a ton. Then he died.

He was buried without religious ceremony. This is the story of Burro Schmidt.

Another Empty Hole

Burro Schmidt was a raging atheist. He was so profane that his burros could not understand him without his cursing. His single motivation in life was to "strike it rich." He was willing to rob himself of friendships, simple pleasures, physical and mental well-being in pursuit of a golden dream as elusive as desert mirages that promise life-giving water but deliver only sand. In that search, he sold his soul and squandered his days in frenzied despair. His moldering bones lie in another hole—this time just six-feet long, three-feet wide, and less than six-feet deep, but they are there! Only the skulking coyotes sing his requiem.

Burro Schmidt would have been forgotten except for writers (and I am one of them) who resurrected his story for its human interest and its obvious moral.

On any Easter morning, hundreds of morbidly curious and pleasure-seeking visitors will brave the rough desert roads to stand before an empty hole which a blasphemous atheist dug in the rock, and they will laugh at his folly and remember him as a fool.

On a rocky hill outside the northern wall of Jerusalem near the place where Jesus died on a bloody cross is a tomb carved out of the solid rock. That tomb is empty. On that same Easter Sunday when hundreds will gather to laugh at the memory of Burro's misspent life, multiplied millions of believers in the crucified, risen Christ will stand figuratively (and a few literally) before His empty tomb and sing, "He lives, he lives, . . . he lives within my heart." They will be lifted to the portals of heaven as they sing. They will go into the world to serve Him. In so doing, they will lay up for themselves in heaven the only imperishable riches this tottering earth affords: treasures of redeemed souls whom they have pointed to their Lord and eternal Savior.

More Precious than Gold

The choice is ours alone to make. We are free moral agents, free to choose and free to use our time. We can spend our lives in pursuit of the material and the sensual, or we can spend them seeking and helping those who need our Christ and—by extension since we belong to Him—our own love.

Contrast the life of a man like Burro with that of another man. He, too, was eighty-two years old when I interviewed him. He stood straight and tall, carrying his years lightly as though they were feathers. Asbel S. Petrey was one of the greatest men I ever met. He, too, had a mine. His mine was the Cumberland Mountains of Kentucky. His treasure was human souls. He was a miner for God: "They shall be mine, saith the Lord of hosts, in that day when I make up my jewels; and I will spare them, as a man spareth his own son that serveth him" (Mal. 3:17).

Many years ago the Home Mission Board of the Southern Baptist Convention sent me into the Cumberland Mountains of Eastern Kentucky to find a veteran preacher named Petrey who had spent fifty years ministering to the hill dwellers—many of them living beyond all roads with the only way to their cabins on mule back. I was to spend three weeks with him, traveling with him over the countryside, interviewing those whom he had served. Then I was to write the story of his life. The project was a joint undertaking of the Southern Baptist Home Mission Board and the Kentucky Board of Missions. My companion in Kentucky was L. O. Griffith, himself a veteran of mountain missions work. The title of my book was *The Prophet of Little Cane Creek.* Just last week I received another request for the book, though it was written nearly forty years ago and has been out of print about thirty. It was a thrilling story, not because of how it was written but because it is the chronicle of a dedicated man's victorious life.

One afternoon, as the long Kentucky twilight was falling, I sat on the porch of the little vine-covered home of Brother Petrey in Hazard, Kentucky. I had set up an old-time wire recorder (tape recorders had not been invented) and recorded my interview with this grand old preacher. Incidentally, I still have that working recorder and the voice of Brother Petrey is still clear and forceful.

I asked my host, "Brother Petrey, what is the

greatest thing that ever happened to you in these fifty years of preaching in the mountains?"

The gray-haired preacher did not hesitate. He answered, "It happened about two weeks ago. Do you see that church building over there?" He pointed to a white spire on a neighboring hill. "That is the Petrey Memorial Baptist Church. I didn't want it named after me, but they did it anyway. Well, a couple of weeks ago, I was the guest at services there. When I stepped inside, I noticed that the ushers had baskets of red roses. They were handing them to everybody except me. I wondered about that. I was escorted to the platform. After some preliminaries, the young pastor stepped forward and said, as he took my arm and helped me to my feet, 'If Brother Petrey is responsible for leading you to Christ, please come up here and pin a rose on him.' "

That selfless missionary preacher paused, and tears misted his eyes. He continued with a tremor in his voice. "They started coming. They came from all over the auditorium. They started pinning roses on me. They pinned them all over my coat, front and back, then down my britches legs, and I stood there feeling like a blooming idiot," he chuckled. Then he grew serious. "But I wouldn't trade those roses for all the gold buried at Fort Knox, for all the coal under these hills, and all the hardwood in their forests. Each rose represented someone, a beloved friend, that I will meet in heaven."

When I heard that this marvelous man of God had

died, I sat back and closed my eyes. I tried to imagine that scene in heaven when he arrived there. I imagined that I could see them coming from every direction, dressed in robes of white, each of them saying, "Thank you, Brother Petrey. Without your guidance, I might never have found the way."

My dear old friend is in that garden of paradise where the roses never fade and friendships never die. With him will be his treasures "where neither moth nor rust doth corrupt, and where thieves do not break through nor steal" (Matt. 6:20).

Golden Nuggets of Time

Humans were not created to spend life in a hole in the ground. They were made to inhabit eternity. This is simply to remind us all that supreme values can be overlooked in our obsession with the trivial. Henry Wadsworth Longfellow reminded us that

> Life is real! Life is earnest!
> And the grave is not its goal;
> Dust thou art, to dust returnest,
> Was not spoken of the soul.

The Golden Nugget of Prayer

Jesus never faced any major decision without praying to his Heavenly Father, yet sometimes that is our last recourse. We should never face a single day without a conference with God. We know that in our hearts and assent to it with our minds, but do we know the daily peace of asking and receiving the direction of the Holy Spirit both in our desires and in our actions? These are days of stress for us all. Personal anxieties seem to multiply with age. Through the activity of the news media, both print and broadcast, we try to carry the troubles of the whole world on our shoulders. We are not, within ourselves, big enough for all that. Paul wrote "The peace of God, which passeth all understanding, shall keep your hearts and minds through Christ Jesus" (Phil. 4:7).

The Golden Nugget of Bible Reading

Most Christians spend more time with the daily newspaper than they do with the Bible—the Word of life. We should read the newspapers; we are not made to be hermits, insulated from our fellowman. We need to read good magazines and books for information and simple pleasure. Does the news we see and hear depress us? There is one Book of Good News. Wouldn't you hate trying to live without the Twenty-third Psalm, the fourteenth chapter of John, the eighth chapter of Romans, and others fitting your every need? Something else—heaven and earth will pass away, but the Word of our God will abide forever. It is the only Book that will. Furthermore, it does not change with the mores of society; it knows nothing of situation ethics; it does not accommodate itself to either the whims or vagaries of people. It is sublime truth and forever to be trusted. We need such immutable guidance in these ever-changing times of nervous uncertainty. Furthermore, the Bible is God's love letter to His children. We must let it indwell our minds and hearts. We all know this, but we are prone to busy ourselves with trivia.

The Golden Nugget of Worship

Private devotions lift our spirits heavenward; so, too, does public worship. This is one major reason Christ instituted His church. Songs of praise bursting from every throat, hearts finely tuned to the message of God as delivered by His faithful servants, quiet observance of the beautiful ordinances of baptism and the Lord's Supper, even joyful worship in tithes and offerings—in all of this we gain the strength for another week. Our cares are laid aside, giving way to tranquillity of spirit. How can we live successfully without that if we are physically able to participate? How, indeed?

Golden Nuggets of Service

Many preachers have pointed out that the small Sea of Galilee is filled constantly with fresh, life-sustaining water because it gives out what it receives. That water flows through a rift sixty-five miles long, but the Jordan itself winds like a snake some two hundred miles in the process. Then the fresh water plunges into the sea called "Dead"—which supports no life. The water dies there, becoming so salty that a human body cannot sink in it. The Dead Sea receives but it never gives out. Those preachers have reminded us that some lives are like the Sea of Galilee, giving out the imparted blessings of God in service to him. Other lives are like the unusable waters of the Dead Sea for one reason: They do not give out what they receive.

There are those, most remembered, who spend themselves in love and good deeds. Empty-minded newspaper columnists label such persons "do-gooders." When their columns are used to wrap dead fish, the so-called do-gooders will be remembered by the millions of struggling souls they have helped.

Through the community service of the various organizations of our church, we reach personally those in the area where we live. Through Christian missions, we reach those in our state, country, and around the world. Part of this is through our financial gifts. It is everlastingly true that: "All that I can hold in my cold, dead hand is what I have given away."

What Can I Do?

• A ten-year-old girl walks down the church aisle and presents her friend to the pastor with the words, "Mary has given her heart to Christ and wants to confess Him as her Savior."

• A woman legally blind walks a mile every day to read large-print books to the residents of a rest home.

• Six beauty operators from a large Texas church go every Thursday to beautify the hair of women residents of a rest home.

• A senior adult department of a small California Baptist church saves money and purchases wheelchairs for crippled and ill needy persons.

• Carpenters, brick and stone masons, plasterers, and plumbers pay their expenses to Brazil to build a church house from foundation to roof in only three weeks. The men come from half a dozen churches in the United States.

• A paralyzed woman confined to her bed for the rest of her life contributes the most of all. She lifts her heart's concerns several times every day in intercessory prayer.

These, and dedicated Christians like them, lay up treasures in heaven's impregnable storehouse. Are you and doing the same?

6
A Time to Love

Dear friends, let us love one another, because love is from God. Everyone who loves is a child of God and knows God, but the unloving know nothing of God. For God is love; and his love was disclosed to us in this, that he sent his only Son into the world to bring us life. The love I speak of is not our love for God, but the love he showed to us in sending his Son as the remedy for the defilement of our sins. If God thus loved us, dear friends, we in turn are bound to love one another (1 John 4:7-11, NEB).

During a revival in a small, Arizona desert town, the pastor and evangelist went to see a service station owner for whom the church had been praying. The man courteously offered them chairs in his office and leaned back in his desk chair to listen. His face had hardened in unconcern. The pastor opened the conversation by pointing out the man's need for Christ. All the while the evangelist sat silent, his eyes taking in every detail of the tiny office.

"I don't believe in God," snapped the man derisively. I could never believe in any God who will permit so much evil in the world when He could stop it. I can't believe in a God who will let this war go on." He gestured toward a large picture on the wall. "That's Tom, my son. He's a marine. He is overseas now, being shot at. He may get killed." His voice choked up. "If there is a God, why does He allow so much hate in the world?"

The evangelist had been studying the large picture of the young marine. The lad wore his uniform proudly. His eyes were clear, and his mouth was upturned in a winsome smile. The evangelist spoke for the first time in this solemn session. "You love Tom very much, don't you?"

The man's reply was quick. "I love him so much I would die for him and just wish that I could."

The evangelist suggested: "You talk about so much hate in the world. Have you ever wondered where love came from? The Bible says, 'God is love.' All love comes from God, not from the law of the jungle. You say that you would die for your son because you love him so much. God, through love, gave His only Son to die on the cross so you and I could live with Him forever. God did that for persons yet unborn."

The man thought for a long moment, and a new light began to shine in his eyes. "I think I'm beginning to understand a little of it now. Go ahead—tell me more. I'm listening."

A few minutes later, he had accepted Christ as Lord and Savior. Where argument, no matter how sound, would have steeled that man's will, God's love broke through.

God Not to Blame

At the height of World War II, a man posed this question for George W. Truett: "If there is a God, why doesn't He stop this war?"

Truett replied, "Perhaps, dear brother, it is because He didn't start it."

The banner in the hands of some protester that reads "War Is Immoral" reflects the murkiness of many minds. War is neither moral nor immoral. The same fuzzy thinking produces the sign "Atomic Bombs Are Immoral." Morality belongs to those with the power to reason. Bombs do not make themselves, neither do they fall by their own design. When we think at all, we know this, but it is our nature to blame anyone or anything except ourselves. The heresy goes all the way back to Eden: "The woman whom thou gavest to be with me" (Gen. 3:12). In other words, "You did it, God, when You made the woman who enticed me to break your commandment; therefore, I am not to blame; you are."

The service station man was not reasoning accurately. In fact, he was not reasoning at all. He was hurt. The son whom he loved might die. The evangelist was able to establish a common bond between the man and God once the man understood God's own heart of love. A greater motivation than fear of

hell is love of God. On this truth, the soul-winner
built.

God so loved us that He gave his Son. If we love
Him, we will give Him ourselves. Furthermore, we
shall love each other. This is not an elective option.
It is a direct command. "This is his commandment,
That we should believe on the name of his Son Jesus
Christ, and love one another" (1 John 3:23). Can
love be commanded? This kind of love can be. It is
a selfless love—a love that seeks no recompense for
itself. It is called by the Greek word *agape*—the no-
blest form of human emotion. This is the kind of
love that should exist throughout the membership
of any church. Paul wrote to the Philippians, "I have
you in my heart" (Phil. 1:7). This is a most interesting verse. No one knows for certain what Paul actually said. The Greek words can read either, "I have
you in my heart" or "you have me in your heart."
This is the relationship that should exist between
the pastor and congregation. It is the relationship
that should exist between individual members on a
one-to-one basis. Where such love exists, the lack of
harmony cannot.

Love in the Home

The most important element in human society is
what is called the nuclear home—father, mother,
and children. This is God's first outreach of love.
God created male and female to supplement each
other. He made them sexually attractive and com-
patible to and with each other with one basic pur-

pose: procreation of the race. No one can deny that sex is ecstatic pleasure to the normal person, but its biological purpose has been to bring into the world children to grow up and reproduce themselves in the *libido* stream of life. This is not to suggest or even to hint that a home cannot be happy without children; nor is it to suggest that the only function of Eve was to produce children. The Bible says that she was to be Adam's "help meet" (Gen. 2:18). In Genesis 2:24, she is called his "wife."

Notwithstanding all this, the primary reason for the existence of the home is children. Since this little book concerns time, let us examine its sequence in the life of the child. Love must play its part in every time frame.

Infancy

This is the period covering the first two years of life. Psychologists tell us what every good parent knows instinctively: The infant needs to be touched, caressed, held, and cuddled. This is the babe's first impression of life. Love now means that anxiety and fear are driven away. If neglected now, the babe is scarred forever.

Childhood

This extends from the third to the twelfth years of life. During this time the child begins to realize a feeling of self-esteem. The child must be subject to discipline, and the wise parent knows how to give it and will unfailingly do so. The growing one must not be over protected but must be guided through some hard knocks from life itself if the child is to learn self-reliance. Through this formative period, children must know the assurance of genuine love. Without such love communicated, all else fails. Furthermore, during this time the child must learn to interact with others. It is a time of jealousy and aggressiveness in territorial protection: "What's mine is mine, and I'll keep it." Cooperation must be demonstrated and taught. The child must be encouraged to share. It is a formidable task for the parent but is the beginning of the child's own outreach of love and can set the pattern for life.

Adolescence

By definition, this is the period between twelve and twenty-one. It is, for the youth and parents involved, a time of storm and stress.

Just ten miles from our home, this morning's newspaper relates, a mother found her thirteen-year-old daughter hanging in a tree. The girl was dead. In the grim, nightmarish week that followed, six other students from Britton Middle School (where the dead girl, Maggie, attended) attempted suicide. Twelve more of her friends planned their own suicides on the Sunday after Maggie's death. I looked at a picture of the beautiful little girl. She was kneeling by the sheep which she had entered as her 4-H Club project at the county fair. She looked as happy as any other girl her age. Who could have guessed at the agonies in her heart which drove her to such an act of desperation? You may already have come to the conclusion that Maggie was the victim of the drug habit. You would be right. This precious girl tied the rope around her own neck, but she was murdered—murdered by the one who sold her the dope. Even then, she was not killed instantly as with a bullet in her head, but she was slowly tortured to death.

In the history of the world, it is doubtful that any age group has known more turmoil of spirit than have the adolescents of our time. Five thousand young people, aged fifteen to twenty-four, kill themselves every year, and five hundred thousand more attempt suicide.

No parents since time began ever faced such a challenge. Without God and His love communicated through them, parents cannot possibly succeed. Drugs, alcohol, premarital sex—these are the three evils busy destroying our young and thereby rotting this land that is not so free. It might be noted, however, that some dedicated parents are helping to grow the strongest children ever to grace the earth. They are, because they have stood its greatest test.

Parents Must Love Each Other

Paul, who may or may not have married, said this —and it is of God—"Let the husband render unto the wife due benevolence: and likewise also the wife unto the husband" (1 Cor. 7:3). That is the formula for a successful marriage, and it proceeds out of mutual respect and love for one another.

I was recently asked to discuss marriage with a group of Christian college students. After my little speech, a student observed: "You have been married going on sixty years." Then she asked: "What is the secret of success in so long a marriage?"

I had no chance to think. I offered a few remarks off the top of my head. The following is a brief digest of my informal remarks:

The primary ingredient in a successful marriage is no secret. It is found in just one all-inclusive word: *love*. This is something more than a marriage contract. It is a genuine heart feeling. Ina and I shared such mutual love, and all else dropped into place. We considered marriage to be a partnership. When it became evident that I didn't have much sense about money, we made an arrangement. She would pay all the bills, keeping all the records. I would simply earn the money. Family counselors tell us that most arguments between husband and wife are not about the opposite sex and such relationships nor about liquor, but about *money*.

My wife has never worked outside the home, and that is most fortunate for us. She did her work, and I did mine. For instance, we had four children, and I never changed a diaper. I wouldn't know which end of the baby to put a diaper on and never tried to find out. (I hold in great esteem the men who were good enough fathers to change diapers. I am wrong, and they are right.)

Since Ina had to help me in church work, going with me in afternoon visitation, I did dry the dishes for her and run the vacuum cleaner once in awhile; but she accepted household tasks as hers and expected, and got, little from me at this point.

We had family "togetherness." We had loving companionship with our children. We took our vacations camping in the mountains, by lakes and streams—even in later life—by the seashore. We helped our growing children to appreciate nature and nature's God. They knew the simple joys of watching the campfire cast flickering lights on the tent walls, then finally dying to bright coals until ultimately only the stars were left to light the night. They all knew the principal constellations and the fables surrounding them. They never caused us serious worry, and today they are all married in homes with as much love and endurance as the one they left. We were, of all parents, most fortunate.

"I have you in my heart." It must be the motto of every member of a happy home. "You have me in your heart" is the flip side of the record.

God Is Love

Millions of books have been written and published describing the attributes of God. Most of them are helpful reading, helping us to understand what God is like. The Bible sums up the whole thought in just three short words: "God is love" (1 John 4:16).

Many of life's experiences seem to contradict this assurance.

Evil Seems to Deny It

War drenches the earth in blood. America does not escape. The service station owner in the beginning of this chapter voiced a common complaint. Fifty-eight thousand of our young men died in the jungles of Vietnam, and tens of thousands are maimed in body and mind for life in a war in which there was no victory. Fifty thousand young American soldiers died in the "police" action in Korea, and the sole result was armed truce with thousands of our soldiers still stationed there after thirty years.

Tragedy Seems to Deny It

A Christian family on the way home from church is smashed by a hit-and-run driver. Father and mother are killed, and two tiny children are left to be reared by an aged grandmother who cannot, herself, live long enough to do it.

Sickness Seems to Deny it

How can God fail to raise up our loved one for whom we have prayed with all the earnestness of our souls? Rabbi Harold S. Kushner has written a book: *When Bad Things Happen to Good People.* It is a small volume, not much longer than this one, but he says that he took fifteen years to write it—ever since he learned that his son Aaron was the victim of the heartbreaking disease progeria. The dedication page of the book says:

IN MEMORY OF
AARON ZEV KUSHNER
1963-1977

And David said, "While the child was yet alive, I fasted and wept: for I said, Who can tell whether God will be gracious to me, that the child may live? But now he is dead, wherefore should I fast? can I bring him back again? I shall go to him, but he shall not return to me" (2 Sam. 12:22-23).

Rabbi Kushner asked this question near the conclusion of the book:

> Are you capable of forgiving and accepting in love a world which has disappointed you by not being perfect, a world in which there is so much unfairness and cruelty, disease and crime, earthquake and accident? Can you forgive its imperfections and love it because it is capable of containing great beauty and goodness, and because it is the only world we have?[1]

To this I would simply add my own comment: This is not all the world we have. We are also citizens of another world toward which we journey—a world where every troubling question will be answered, every longing satisfied, and no little boy will grow old before his time, and pain and tears will be no more. Here is where God's love finally leads us.

In the meantime, we who partake of the very nature of God can busy ourselves on life's brief journey by communicating His love to those who might thereby come to know Him, too.

Dr. W. O. Carver inscribed his book *The Glory of God in the Christian Calling* to me in this manner. He wrote: "Eph. 3:2 Grace through me on its way to you." Love is God's grace in action. Can we paraphrase the autograph of Dr. Carver to read, "Love from me on its way to you"? I think that we can. Will you join me in trying to practice it more consistently?

Note

1. Harold S. Kushner, *When Bad Things Happen to Good People* (New York: Schocken Books, 1981), pp. 147-148.

7

A Time to Relax

We richly endowed Americans have more leisure-time than any other people on the earth. The question is: Have we learned how to use it? Dr. Geoffrey Godby, a professor in Pennsylvania State University's Parks and Recreational Department says, "We kind of have a frantic quality about our leisure." He is the author of a book, *Leisure in Your Life: An Exploration.*

He is right. Have you ever watched people trying to have a good time? They play as though they were fighting the decisive battle of a global war. They watch sports, especially bodily contact sports, the same frenzied way. There is a certain intensity about it that is all-pervading. Otherwise level-minded persons become, for awhile, raving lunatics.

The 1985 Super Bowl game was played in Stanford Stadium, less than twenty miles from our home. Day after day, the Bay-area newspapers hyped up the game. We were deluged by column after column about how much each player weighed, what he liked to eat, his accumulated yardage for the last season, *ad nauseum, ad infinitum.* Joe Montana, Forty-niners' quarterback, and his counterpart, Dan Marino, Dolphins' quarterback, sent "The Gipper" (President Ronald Reagan) to the showers. There was just one state of the Union: Stanford Stadium.

Finally, THE GAME! The whole world knows how it ended: Forty-niners 38—Dolphins 16!

The game was great. I enjoyed every minute of it—over the "big eye" in the living room. It didn't cost me a single thing except a stomach ache from too much coffee. But there were many who had spent more than one thousand dollars just to get a stadium seat. One man had traded his boat worth several thousand dollars to sit on a hard bench with his knees in another fellow's back for three hours. In addition, he lost his cap when somebody grabbed it off his head and threw it away.

There was celebration in San Francisco that night! The fans were having great fun. Cars were overturned. Some were set on fire. Drunkenness was everywhere; gross immorality was practiced by some on the streets. Hundreds suffered minor injuries, and hundreds more were arrested.

It took several days and more than $100,000 to get the Stanford Stadium cleaned up. Tons of trash were hauled away. A wonderful time was had by all. No one would have missed it for the world.

Take a walk along any ocean beach. Ten thousand almost naked bodies lie burning on the sands; twenty swimmers are in the water. They are really the only ones having any pleasure. The others are simply kidding themselves into thinking they are.

We go out after pleasure as though our very lives depended on our finding it RIGHT NOW. Our search is feverish; our obsession, pitiful. More often than not, we come back with our exhaustion increased and our frustration compounded.

Can You Relax?

Ike knew how. Let me tell you about Ike. The hour I first met him, I came to like him. As I began to know him better, my liking became tinged with envy. Ike knew how to turn loose of everything, including himself. He relaxed all over—no tenseness in mind nor body. He knew how to play, not with a frenetic expenditure of energy but with complete enjoyment. The Bible does not condemn the kind of envy that I felt for Ike. My friend was an Irish setter. He was the color of a fire engine and weighed in at seventy pounds. He is now in his own happy hunting ground.

Ike belonged to our daughter Lila Belle and her family. They live in a country house near Southern Pines, North Carolina. It is in the sand hills country. The hills are covered with a dozen kinds of trees and hundreds of different kinds of flowers. I like to take a path that leads some two miles through the stands of loblolly pines, the woods garnished with flowering dogwoods, shining whitely against a background of redbuds in a curtain of color. Ike always went with me. While I walked the crooked trail, Ike loped off to one side. His long body seemed to float through the air and seemed to be jointed in the middle. I wondered how he could keep from breaking in two.

Ike didn't say much. Now and then he barked at a squirrel which darted up the trunk of an oak and sat on a limb, talking back in a language that seemed to be a little profane. Ike, though, had nothing to say to me. He left me undisturbed in my thoughts, not because he was unfriendly but because he respected my moods. He was having his dog fun, and I was having my man kind. We understood each other perfectly.

Never have I felt more relaxed myself than when I wandered through the woods with my friend Ike. Such hours are the stuff of delightful dreams. They refresh the soul. They make life more worth the living. Cares are forgotten; frustrations drop away like a tattered garment. Then we are ready for another day and can meet it confidently.

When I get all tensed up with nerves that go jinglejangle, I think of Ike and am thankful that I got to know him. "But," you say, "he was only a dog. He never accomplished anything."

Ike accomplished what some persons never do even if they *are* called human. He brought happiness to everyone who knew him. That could have been written on his tombstone. I wish it could be written on mine. In this, too, I envy him.

Relax with a Hobby

I asked a pastor friend what he did for relaxation. His answer was, "I read." When I asked him what he read, he said, "Books on theology. Right now I am reading a book on antinomianism."

"Aunty who?" I asked.

"Antinomianism."

"Who wrote it—Erle Stanley Gardner?"

"Is he a professor?" asked my friend. Of course we were kidding, and no blood was shed. Who am I to say what relaxes my pastor friend? Maybe he reads such books in order to go to sleep. They would have that effect on me. I wouldn't read a whole book on antinomianism unless it were an entrance requirement for heaven; even then, I would have to think about it.

A hobby furnishes a welcome change of pace. The old routine is broken and that within itself is rest for weary minds and bodies. Most of us, fortunately, do have hobbies. We gain much pleasure from them. We also develop skills which are useful in broader ways. I believe that a hobby that helps us physically is more beneficial than one that is sedentary. That is just my opinion, of course. For instance I have another friend who collected stamps. His collection, when he showed it to me, was worth in excess of $10,000. Although it meant much to him, he expected to sell it in order to pay his daughter's beginning college year. Just before she was graduated from high school, burglars broke into his home and took the stamp collection along with many other valuable things. The collection was not insured.

My son-in-law Bob is a jogger. He expects to jog all the way to the pearly gates. He is never happier than when he is jogging along at 4:30 in the morning with the cold wind in his face. No burglar can ever steal away his health. No thief can rob him of his stronger heart nor wither his thighs and calves nor make his lungs wheeze in pain. It would kill me to try what he does day after day come rain or shine, hail or snow, but he loves every moment of it.

My old fishing buddy, Dave Molencupp, told me about a trip that he made to Oregon. He expected to fill his creel every day with rainbow trout. He drove a round trip of nine hundred miles and caught one fish, a rainbow that was six inches long. "But that little devil sure put up a fight," he said. "It was worth every dollar and every minute of the trip."

I don't have to explain that to any dyed-in-the-wool fisher person. For anyone else, though, a relaxing hobby is not a battle for a certain victory but an attitude of mind. We simply do best what we enjoy doing.

Sometimes a hobby, though engaged in for a different purpose, issues a benefit to others. My wife and I have been associated with two remarkable women at three chautauquas at Glorieta (Senior Adult Conferences). Sarah Loyd and Charlotte Hart are from Green Acres Baptist Church, Tyler, Texas. Their hobby is handwork—many kinds.

They are proficient in ceramics, painting, needle-work, beadwork (you name it; they can make it). These years they have supervised the popular Crafts Workshop program at the chautauquas.

At home, the hobby has been put to missionary use. The women of the church, under their direction, have produced hundreds of needed articles for area rest homes and the mission operated by the Green Acres Church in Mexico. Others have shared this experience. Simple hobbies have led to pleasurable avenues of lasting, loving service. Thus, there are double rewards.

The list of hobbies available to anyone today is as varied as human personality. It is too long to be included here. One thing more needs to be said. One should cultivate a hobby early in life. Proficiency makes for enjoyment.

The Universe Around Us

God has made for our quiet enjoyment a most beautiful world. It is all around us. Pick that hated dandelion out of your lawn, and before you throw it away, take a good look at it. Did you ever see a more glorious golden crown? How about the shy little violet peeping out from the shadow of a rock? It may be blooming within a patch of snow, but it laughs happily up at your face. Walk through the woods, slowly. Joyce Kilmer said, "Poems are made by fools like me,/But only God can make a tree."

Most workers in modern-day America enjoy a five-day week with a two-week vacation once a year.

That is a wealth of leisure time—well spent. Such precious hours can be squandered by haste. The only way to enjoy the delights of the natural world is to *take your time.* Many people pursue their vacations at such a pace that they see little and remember less. If they travel by auto (as most do), their primary concern seems to be the miles traveled each day. All that remains in their minds is a blur. How many flowers can you see even at fifty-five miles per hour? How many birds can you hear singing above the roar of an automobile engine? How many stars can you see through the roof of your car?

Come . . . and Rest Awhile

The disciples had brought word to Jesus of the death of John the Baptist, the man who loved God so much that he feared no man on earth. They had obtained the body at Machaerus prison and had placed it lovingly in a tomb. Dissolute Herod and his equally dissolute women had wrought their vengeance. The lips that had condemned their sin would never speak again.

This was crushing news to Jesus. John, the forerunner who had proclaimed Him as the Lamb of God, was also His blood-related kinsman, so the burden was doubly heavy. The Master had suffered another heartbreak. He had gone back to Nazareth, His boyhood home, to carry the news of salvation, but they that were "his own received him not" (John 1:11).

The disciples, too, were physically and mentally fatigued.

With his own weariness showing, Jesus said, "Come ye yourselves apart into a desert place, and rest a while" (Mark 6:31).

It was not to be. In order to escape the pressing crowds, the Master and His disciples crossed over the little sea by boat, but clamoring people met them on the other shore. Jesus, the Bible says, had "compassion on the multitude" (Mark 8:2). He forfeited His rest in order to minister to them. It sometimes happens that way with us. "What do you consider the greatest gift you can give your students?" I once asked a popular college professor. His answer was quick, "My time."

A strange thought came to me as I sat that day in my little temple in the rocks described in the first chapter. It hinged around the invitation Jesus issued to His disciples and was probably prompted by my own desert experience. I thought: *I wish I could have sat on the grass of the mountain called the Horns of Hattin and heard the Master preach. I wish I could have heard Him pray for me—I was in that prayer in the seventeenth chapter of John—I wish I could have slipped into that upper room and listened, sacred though the moment was. I wish I could have heard Him sing.* Before the betrayal, Matthew says, "When they had sung an hymn, they went out into the Mount of Olives." Then I had another wish: *I wished that I could have gone out into the desert alone with my Lord, just the two of us.*

My train of thought climaxed. We had done just

that. We who love Him do not—cannot—go anywhere without Him. This is ultimate relaxation. This is quietness of the spirit, our renewal, our re-creation.

8
A Time to Laugh

The church business meeting had turned ugly. The pastor was ashamed, and other members were heartsick. What was the trouble all about? It was a long time ago, and "much water has passed under the bridge since then." No one remembers exactly what the fuss was about. Some say that the argument arose about whether the church would install ceiling fans in the auditorium. The people already had nice hand-operated fans supplied by the local mortuary advertising its terminal services. One man, who argued loudly, insisted that the trouble arose over the decision to buy a piano for one of the Sunday School departments. Although he added to the trouble that night, he can't remember why he got so all-fired worked up about it.

Finally, before any blows were struck or any blood was splattered on the pews, a deacon arose and cleared his throat. When that deacon cleared his throat, it always brought instantaneous silence to the congregation. He was a long, tall "drink of water" with an adam's apple that bounced up and down like a yo-yo when he talked. "Naow brethren," he said, "I once had an old hawg . . ."

I was a young preacher then, and I don't remember how that "hawg" entered the church business meeting, but I welcomed him. A ripple of laughter started and spread until most of the parishioners were happy again. I have seen that happen in many denominational meetings, and even years ago in the huge Southern Baptist Convention where twenty thousand messengers were calmed down when the moderator told a funny story. *Robert's Rules of Order* had to take a back seat while humor stole the show.

You have seen it too. A sprinkle of laughter was the oil that smoothed troubled waters. It can also smooth the troubled waters of the soul. We can laugh our troubles away when anger and frustration simply intensify them.

Leslie D. Weatherhead, the late London preacher, said, "Humor is one of the best solvents in the world for the grit of irritation that gets into the cogs of life these days, and the man who can laugh at himself as well as others will be among the last casualties in the war of nerves."[1]

I shall leave it to the trained psychologists to guess whether such an attribute is a gift of birth. If that is the only way it can be acquired, some of us are in bad shape. We can't go back and rebirth ourselves. I am of the opinion that, regardless of inherited genes, we can train ourselves to see the lighter side of life. If we cannot, we are doomed to misery.

Life, as the old country song goes, would certainly

be "teejus." I am not saying that we should all be comedians. It is not the same. Some of the most tedious performers I ever see or hear are the "stand-up" comics reciting obnoxious jokes someone else has written. And to think that scads of people pay good money to be "entertained" by them. A moth-eaten old alley cat yowling at the garbage can be funnier. And that canned laughter on TV comic shows (double meaning here)! Even the laughter of a pack of hyenas would be more realistic. "Tain't funny, McGee." (Neither is that crack funny to anyone under fifty.)

No, I am talking about genuine humor—seeing the laughable as we wend our way over many rocky roads.

The Best Medicine

My good friend T. J. DuBose had a serious heart attack and was taken to the hospital to intensive care. He was a metropolitan missions director and a member of our church. I went to see him one day after he was taken from the intensive care unit. He greeted me with his characteristic wide grin. Before long we were having a fantastic time, joking and laughing together.

Right in front of his door and across the hall, two nurses sat at a table. When they heard the laughter, they frowned and held a consultation with each other, looking up at me (in plain sight) all the while. Finally the one who seemed to be in charge left the table and came into T. J.'s room. She stared at me with eyes like laser beams. "I let you in because you are a pastor and therefore privileged. I must ask you to leave now. You may be complicating the recovery of the patient."

T. J. protested. "Oh, no! He gave me the medicine I needed."

"He gave you medicine?" the nurse almost screamed. Then, addressing me, she yelled, "You had no right to give him any medicine at all. Only the physician can do that. What did you give him?"

The patient laughed at her; he laughed at me, then laughed at the situation itself. "Keep your shirt on," he advised the nurse. "Haven't you read in the Bible that 'a merry heart doeth good like a medicine'? Here, I'll read it to you." He reached for his Bible. The nurse softened her stance—a little. A smile began to form on her lips. She turned to me with a broad wink and said, "Go ahead and kill 'im." Then out she went. Out I went, too, in a moment.

This is not to criticize the nurse. She acted professionally and responsibly. Heart attacks are treacherous. They are not to be trifled with or laughed at. On the other hand, my friend was up and about in two more days. He lived another year and died of causes unrelated to the heart attack. I brought the message at memorial services for him. I paid him a high tribute, "He was a *gentle*man." He was. For him to have harmed anyone intentionally was unthinkable. I miss his explosive laughter.

That reminds me. Have I told you about my operation? Skip this if you don't want to read about it.

If you have had an operation, you would tell me about it. I wouldn't hear a single word. I would be sitting on the edge of my seat waiting for you to finish so I could tell you about mine.

Anyway, after I had been retired four years, I had a series of heart attacks and then had open-heart surgery with a triple arterial bypass. That's all I am going to tell you about it except to tell about two of my visitors. The first was a beautiful girl of about twenty. We had known her most of her life. She came to see me and stopped just inside the doorway. She just stood there pointing. I had an oxygen tube taped to my nose, tubes in both arms, various electrodes fastened to my body for monitoring purposes. I was a mess. "Are you getting ready to take off for the moon?" asked my pretty visitor. Then she came over to my bed, brushed the plastic tube away from my face, and kissed me right on the lips. Now, I'll admit to being old, but I would have to be dead not to get stirred up by that procedure. When my heart-stopping visitor left the room, she again paused at the doorway and pointed. "You look like the very devil," she said and left.

The nurse came in right on the girl's heels. I told her what had happened. She, too, was very pretty, and I had already told her so. She said, "If you are hinting that I do the same, forget it. That is way beyond my call to duty." She stopped with the thermometer in front of my open mouth and said, "After what you have just told me, I'm afraid your temperature will register 110." Then, when she had read the thermometer three minutes later, she said, "You are a very sick man. It reads normal. But you still look like the devil," she said and flounced out of the room.

Now let me tell you about my next visitor (though I'd like to forget him). He was a tall, funeral sort of man like the Hollywood version of the Protestant minister. Every hair on his head lay exactly in place. He was dressed in black and carried a five-pound black Bible. I had never met him before. He came to my bed, grabbed my hand, and pumped it vigorously. Every stitch of my poor, lacerated flesh screamed.

"I am the Reverend H. William Casey" (not his real name). "This is my day to visit the hospital." (He was right about that; he was visiting the *hospital*.) "How are you getting along, my brother?" (He didn't know me from Adam's off-ox, so he didn't know that I had been preaching most of his life). I knew enough to answer his halfhearted question about my welfare with just one word, and it was probably a lie. "Fine," I said.

The next thing the preacher asked was, "Are you a Christian?" This time I used two words, and they were the truth, "I am."

"Fine," said the sanctimonious character. "I will now read to you from the Bible and will say a prayer for you." He read 1 Corinthians 15:50-58 and his voice lingered on the word "corruptible" a little too long to suit me. Then, holding my hand again, he prayed that I might be "resigned" to my fate. He left me wondering whether he was trying to get me into heaven or was simply assigning me to a different place.

I had probably preached hundreds of sermons during which I had quoted that precious Scripture, and it just might have had some application to my hospitalization, but I needed more the humor of my lovely female visitor and the sympathetic, laughing nurse than I did the visit from the cleric in black.

Laughter Makes Us Companionable

One of the funniest, most scholarly and eloquent men I ever knew was W. A. Carleton, widely known church historian, academic dean and assistant president of Golden Gate Baptist Theological Seminary in Mill Valley, California.

He was one of the best friends I ever had. His middle name was Augustus, and even casual acquaintances called him Gus.

During a religious convention several years ago, I picked up a rental car to be delivered in San Francisco. The rental company would pay for the gas and oil, and I would just pay one dollar—for insurance purposes, I suppose. I invited my friend Gus to drive back with me to Berkeley where the seminary was then located. He demurred at first because he had been involved in a car accident a short time before and had suffered severe neck injuries. Finally he agreed to ride with me one day if I would then put him on a train for the coast. Instead, I delivered him safely to his front door in Berkeley. We had too much fun together to break it up.

Gus would launch out on a humorous story, usually concerning himself, that would be so hilarious my sides would hurt from laughing. His superb narration could make historic church figures come alive again.

As we tooled along the Nevada desert at seventy-five miles per hour (long before the "double-nickel" speed limit), Gus regaled me with the story of Balthasar Hubmaier. Up to that time the old Swiss reformer had been nothing much more than a name to me. Gus put him right in the back of our station wagon. I think that Gus was writing a book about the great Anabaptist and was trying out the chapters on me. The life of Hubmaier ended in tragedy. He was burned at the stake, and his wife was drowned. Even so, my friend found lighter moments to discuss. I was fascinated.

We passed through the little town of Winnemucca without ever seeing it. About twenty miles west of there, the station wagon gave a gurgling sort of gasp, and the engine gave up the ghost. We were out of gas. Just before this sad event occurred, Gus asked, "Are you tired of hearing about Hubmaier?" Just to bedevil him, I said, "I know all about Balthasar Hubmaier. I know more about Balthasar Hubmaier than Balthasar Hubmaier knew about Balthasar Hubmaier. Just one thing I want to know. How do you spell his name?"

"How would I know?" yelled Gus. "Do you think I know *everything?*"

The engine may have died laughing. I said, "It's all your fault. I had intended gassing up in Winnemucca, but you got me so strung out with that story that I never thought about it."

The wind blew stinging sand in my face as I got out of the car. Before I closed the door, I said, "I should get back in three or four days. Can you do without food that long?"

"Are you going to stand there jabbering three days? Get along with ye."

I closed the door as Gus pulled his coat up over his ears, but he was really concerned. I left the seminary professor sitting there all humped up like a little boy.

Fortunately a pickup stopped within fifty feet. I waved at Gus and was on my way. The pickup, containing a man and his wife, took me all the way to a gas station—about ten miles. I was lucky enough to get a ride back and was gone just about one hour.

When we stopped in Reno, Gus and I started to cross the street to a little cafe. He held on to my arm, and I thought it was a show of affection. It was partly that, but then I realized that my friend was losing his eyesight. I had forgotten all about that. He was holding to me for protection in crossing the busy street. Here was a scholar, a man of books. He not only studied them but also wrote them, and he was going blind! Yet he could make fun of his growing handicap. Truly, "A merry heart doeth good."

A Sense of Humor Makes Us More Lovable

We had a college friend. He, too, was named T. J.—T. J. Gamble. He was a big man in every way, over six-feet tall, weighed more than 200 pounds— muscle, not fat. He had a square face like that of George Truett. I was in awe of him. He was one of the most Christlike men I ever knew. There was nothing sanctimonious about him. He was just good as any man can be. I felt uncomfortable with him until one day late in our lives he told me a story. I was never in awe of him again, and I loved him more.

T. J. had preached the Sunday before in a medium-sized New Mexico church. The auditorium had a balcony. A boy about ten had slipped unnoticed into the otherwise empty balcony just as services began. He half sprawled over the balcony rail. Right beneath him sat an old man. About halfway through the visiting pastor's sermon, the old man went to sleep. The kid noticed that the old fellow would lean back, and his mouth would fly open. The old man would straighten up, and before long, the same thing would happen again. The kid had a sack of "goobers"—shelled peanuts that look like brown pebbles. Every time the old man's head came back and his mouth opened, the mean little kid aimed carefully and dropped a peanut at the open mouth. He kept missing. Finally, he took careful aim as though through a Norden bombsight—bull's-eye! The old fellow gagged and came upright, gagging and spitting. The kid leaned back with great satisfaction. Mission accomplished!

T. J. said, "I got so interested in watching what the kid was doing that my sermon went right out the window. I am ashamed of it, but I found myself praying that the kid would hit his target, so I could get on with my sermon!"

I was never afraid of T. J. Gamble again. All three of these great men are in heaven now, and if any more joy can be added to that glorious place, they have added it.

Did Jesus Laugh?

There is no mention in the Bible of Jesus laughing out loud. He was described by Isaiah as a "man of sorrows, and acquainted with grief" (53:3). He was, but that was not all that He was. He was a man of great joy. He was in every sense of the word a real man. He was a real man physically. He walked seventy miles over a rocky road to be baptized. He walked from Peraea to Bethany, some twenty-five miles, in order to raise Lazarus from the dead. He was such a man that rough, hardhanded fishermen gave up their nets and their livelihood to follow Him. Some have even suggested that there was the hint of humor in His invitation, "Come after me and I will make you fishers of men." Why be satisfied with lesser trophies? I have been a fisherman nearly all of my life. I never knew a fisherman who could not laugh—except when a big one got away!

Jesus liked social events. He liked being with people in the ordinary, lighter times of life. His first miracle was performed at the wedding in Cana when, as an old-time preacher put it, "The water blushed in the presence of the Lord and turned into wine."

Jesus used humor in His preaching. Consider His story of the pompous gentleman who strained at a gnat and swallowed a camel, humps and all. Then there was the fellow who picked a splinter out of another's eye but had a two-by-four unnoticed in his own. Then there was the man who hired a brass band to go with him playing loudly as he delivered a thanksgiving basket to the poor (at least that is the sense of it).

When word was brought by the disciples that Herod sought the life of Jesus, Jesus said, "Go ye, and tell that fox" (Luke 13:32). Tell him what? That Jesus would act according to God's plan, not Herod's.

Then, I personally like what He called James and John, two of His special friends. When the Samaritans would not welcome them, these two brothers blew fire from their own nostrils and wanted Jesus to call down fire from heaven to incinerate them. Thereafter, Jesus called them Boanerges—"sons of thunder" (Mark 3:17). There was more, but this is enough to show that Jesus could smile enough to attract the roughest men and the gentlest of little children.

The bumper sticker is right: SMILE. GOD LOVES YOU.

Note

1. Leslie D. Weatherhead, *This Is the Victory* (New York: Abingdon-Cokesbury Press, 1941), p.

9
A Time for Tears

"Joy to the world! the Lord is come."

The plinking notes started as I opened a Christmas card buried among others from all parts of the country. Since we have lived for many years in what is known throughout the world as Silicon Valley in California, I at least have a nodding acquaintance with electronic storage chips. Such a tiny chip, activated by a microswitch invisible to my eyes, tinkled up at me from between the covers of an ordinary greeting card. My first reaction was one of wonder. My second was amazement that such a startling technological achievement would be put to such a trivial use. My last reaction was not mental but heart response. The little chip sang no words to me; they sang themselves in my soul. The lowly shepherds first heard the joyful news from angel voices above the bleak Judean desert. Every Christian has heard them since. They are the melody of earth and heaven, the eternal song of hope.

Christmas is a time of joy in the hearts of all believers in the Son of God—the incarnate Word of life. He came that death might be turned into victory. That was the glorious thought which finally surfaced in my mind when it struggled with the saddening word of the very next card I opened. It told of the death of one of my closest friends of half a century. Burning, unchecked tears blurred the handwritten words for me, and my eyes seemed scalded as I shut them tightly. Helene had written of the death of Colonel Wilfred McCormick, her beloved husband whom I loved in a different way. After the shock had tempered into the dull pain of continuing sorrow, I lost myself in bittersweet memory.

You know the feeling; we all do. Death strikes, and we cry. We are better off if we do so. The psyche suffers if we bottle up our tears. The shortest verse in the Bible is also the longest of all: "Jesus wept" (John 11:35). He wept because two sisters did. He weeps with you and me when our own tears flow. The tears of Jesus are timeless. Two thousand years have not quenched them.

We do not live long in this world before we cry out before the mystery of death. I have read somewhere that children do not feel grief as deeply as do grown-ups. That is not a pronouncement of psychological wisdom; it is an arrogant assumption.

My wife and I visited Tahlequah, Oklahoma. I had not been there is sixty years. As we drove around, happy recollections seeped into my mind. We stopped at the little creek where, as an eight-year-old boy, I had fished for crawdads with the red-

skinned sons of a Cherokee chief. I pointed to a
crawdad lying still under the riffles and told Ina that
it had not moved in sixty years. I said, "His tail
would sure taste good roasted on a piece of wire."
My wife's shuddering reply was "Ugh." The same
old grapevine hung over the pool where it used to
swing when we kids went skinny-dipping in the old
swimming hole (at least it looked just like it). Then
we drove by a large white house set back in an ex-
panse of lawn garnished by towering oaks. A thump
of sorrow touched my breast. Sixty years fled into
their tomb only to be resurrected in my memory. I
remembered the funeral in that house of a little
classmate of mine named Helen. It was my very first
brush with death. As I slowed my car that day of the
long-delayed visit, a far-off scene reappeared in my
mind. I saw again the pretty face of my little friend,
her eyes closed, and her usual smile drained from
her lips. I shed no tears, but I wept inside.

Something else: We never grow beyond the age
of tears, not while we walk the earth. If we could no
longer cry, we could no longer serve. Paul prayed
that he might know Jesus in the fellowship of suffering (Phil. 3:10). Paul also held out the promise that
if we suffer with Him, we shall be glorified with Him
(Rom. 8:17). Isaiah, the prince of prophets, described the one who is undoubtedly the Christ as a
"man of sorrows, and acqainted with grief" (53:3).
Thus we are bound together by sorrow and more
closely to Him in common ties of grief. Let us not

be ashamed when we feel our tears falling under the weight of unutterable sadness.

We sing with our minds the words of the old song:

Does Jesus care when I've said "good-bye"
  To the dearest on earth to me?

And our hearts are made to answer:

O yes, He cares, I know He cares,
  His heart is touched with my grief;
When the days are weary,
  The long night dreary,
  I know my Savior cares.

My wife and I were sitting in the beautiful auditorium during a conference for senior adults at Glorieta, New Mexico. The conference leader asked, "How many of you have lost husband or wife and are living alone? Would you please stand?" I looked around. Of the eleven hundred present, more than nine hundred stood. My eyes flooded with tears. I reached over and caught my wife's hand in my own. In 1987, one year after this book's scheduled publication, my beloved wife and I will have been married sixty years—if we both live. I dared not look at the sad faces around us. Lonely hearts!

Many of us have reached the age when we have more friends in heaven than we have on earth. Every year we lose more who for a time were a part of us; and when they died, a part of us died with them. Do you mind if I introduce you to three of my friends? They had been my friends more than fifty years when death took them from me. I have a more valid reason than just paying tribute to them. I could have filled these pages with dozens of stories about other friends whom I have loved and lost for a while. It is not simply because the deaths of these three friends came so close together but because their lives teach something special in different ways. One was a literary man, one was a woman, and the other was the best friend I ever had. I would like you to know why.

I first met Wilfred McCormick when I was editor of a weekly newspaper in Hagerman, New Mexico. Wilfred, a graduate of Medill School of Journalism, Northwestern University, Evanston, Illinois, had educated himself to become a professional writer. He realized his ambition. "At the time of his death," said an article in an Albuquerque newspaper, "he was believed to have had more hardcover novels in the libraries and schools than any other author."

If you look in your church library on the shelf for boys, you will probably find one or more of his books. They were promoted by Christian book stores all over the country.

Since I was a writer of sorts, it was natural for Wilfred and me to become friends. I understood him. I shared his dreams. Fifty-five years later, we were still good friends.

Wilfred first started writing Western pulp-magazine stories and sold several. He wanted to write for slick paper magazines and could have papered a wall with rejection slips. His first book was *The Three-Two*

Pitch, printed in 1948. It was the first of many books about a small-town baseball team captained by Bronc Burnett, a young man with high moral values combined with baseball savvy. The setting was a small town called Sonora but identifiable as Hagerman. Townspeople whom we knew were also identifiable characters (the editor of the weekly paper was named Dye). Wilfred wrote series of books on baseball, basketball, football, and Boy Scouts. The sports books were chock full of solid coaching tips and emphasized good sportsmanship.

Wilfred was my hunting and fishing partner. We hunted big game in some of the most rugged country in America. In those days, we were both tireless. We actually wore out our heavy boots on one such trip. We not only walked hundreds of miles together but also had rich philosophical discussions around lonely campfires far beyond all trails where the only other light was that of the glittering stars—campfires in the Indians' happy hunting ground.

The last time I saw my friend was shortly before his death. He was going blind. My trail partner, who once rated as expert rifleman and whose eyes were good enough for him to see a fast-curving ball and knock it over the fence, was but a shadow of his former self. Now, he is not even a shadow, but he is a blessed memory.

The Albuquerque Journal pointed out in the story of his death that Wilfred was a retired colonel in the United States Army in World War II; he is listed in *Who's Who in America* and *Who's Who in the World.* He was an active civic leader, held many offices in the Rotary Club, such as president and district governor, and was elected Paul Harris Fellow in 1973.

The one great lesson Wilfred McCormick taught me was this: Never give up. He was a *man.* I shall always miss him.

"Joy to the world" sang the electronic Christmas card, but the Christmas before Wilfred's death, Ina's little eighty-four-year-old Aunt Ruth died of cancer in the same city where Wilfred then lived— Albuquerque, New Mexico. They knew each other well. Ruth was active in the Altrusa Club of professional women.

Ina and I had visited with Ruth in her lovely home one month before her death. She had been lively then, could walk as fast as I could, and farther than I cared to. She was feeling some back pain, though she said little about it. When we left, she promised to see a doctor. She did so, and he gave her six months to live. She lived just twenty-five days.

Ina flew back from our home in California to be with Ruth in the last days of her illness. I followed in my Jeep. I was held up overnight twice because of roads made impassable by snow and storms. At her request, Ruth had been transferred from the hospital to her home where she was receiving hospice care. By the time I arrived, she was lucid only a few moments now and then. When I bent over my friend of fifty-six years, she said her last words to me. She whispered, with a brave attempt at a smile,

"You old so and so," then lapsed into a coma. Those may seem strange words for me to treasure, but they somehow meant more to me than anything else she could have said. I had one last glimpse of her carefree self as I had known her through the years.

Ruth was no blood relative of mine—to love me because of filial duty. Instead, she was a friend for the sake of friendship—a lifetime treasure. She was another with whom I had walked scores of miles, most of it in beautiful country, for she, too, loved the mountains. She was alive to the song of birds, the beauty of the flowers, the limitless sky. Ruth, Ina, and I went camping many times. Ruth did not fish, but while I fished, she sat on the bank of the stream or lake watching the sparkle of the sunlit waters. The three of us made several long trips together with me driving either in our car or hers. She paid all expenses at her own insistence since she had a substantial amount of money, and I had little. On one such trip, we crossed Canada to Banff, Jasper, and Vancouver Island. The last long trip was down the length of the Baja California peninsula, then across the Sea of Cortez by ferry and back up the Mexican mainland to California and New Mexico. There were no tensions among us, no arguments, just sheer pleasure.

More than a half-century ago, while I was pastor of First Baptist Church, Las Cruces, New Mexico, Ruth, as usual, took her vacation with us. She was then the head of a large abstract and title company in Albuquerque.

My little friend and I drove out to the Organ Mountains, nine miles east of Las Cruces. We followed a gravel road to the ranch house of Jim Cox. The area is now a part of the White Sands Proving Ground, and such a trip as we made then would probably be forbidden now. We took a trail from the corral up the east side of the mountain toward the nine-thousand-foot high summit. In early afternoon, we sat down to rest. It was a lazy sort of day. The air was balmy, and the turquoise sky stretched from our mountain to the bluish Sacramentos, some seventy miles to the east. Ruth lay back on the grassy slope, looking upward toward the white clouds sailing majestically across the waveless sea above. She said, quietly, "Aren't they the most beautiful things you ever saw? They are like sailing ships." I looked at her face rather than at the clouds. Although her face was plain and sharp featured, in that moment she was beautiful. I leaned over, and before she could stop me, I kissed her. I quickly learned better. "Now, just cut that out," she said firmly but not unkindly.

I was alone in the room with Ruth when she died without a sound, without a murmur. When I realized that she was gone, I leaned over and kissed her on her emaciated cheek. "Good-bye, little Ruth," I whispered. This time she did not object.

Peris Woodruff was the best friend I ever had. We were classmates in Albuquerque High School and were both fifteen years old. One Sunday afternoon, Peris came out to the sandlot ball diamond where I was doing a poor job at third base. He invited me to go with him to the revival at First Baptist Church that night. "You are not doing very well out here anyway," he said with that little sideways quirk of the lips I remember so well.

"I don't want to go," I said, truthfully. I had never been in a Baptist church in my life.

Peris always was very persuasive. He talked me into going.

Mr. Woodruff, Peris's father, was the associate pastor of the church and led the singing. I don't remember the evangelist nor what he preached about. What I do remember most vividly is that when the invitation was given, Peris put his arm around my shoulders. "Why don't you give your heart to Christ?" He said a little more, and his voice was trembling with emotion. I could feel his love for me. It touched my heart. Still I refused to surrender. Then Peris said, "If you want me to, I'll walk down the aisle with you."

By that time Someone greater than my friend Peris had reached my heart. The Holy Spirit spoke to me. I realized that I was a sinner and needed God. My objections were suddenly swept away, and I said, "I can make it by myself."

I walked down and gave my heart to God and my

hand to Pastor T. F. Harvey. I was safe in the arms
of Christ forever.

Six months later (I was hard to convince that I
should be a Baptist), Brother Harvey baptized me.
Then one night, Brother Harvey preached on
"What is that in thine hand?" (Ex. 4:2). He gave the
invitation, and twenty-two young people surren-
dered for special Christian service. Among them
were Peris Woodruff, Russell Goff (who became one
of New Mexico's most successful pastors), and I.
Standing by my side was a girl named Ina. We were
not going together then, but she has walked by my
side nearly sixty years.

That is why I say that Peris Woodruff was the best
friend I ever had on the earth: He turned me toward
Jesus. Because of Peris, I found my way to eternal
life.

I had visited with Peris and his lovely wife Juanita
in their home in Edmonds, Washington. I was on my
way back from a senior adult conference at Mount
Baker Assembly Grounds. Peris had just been
released from a Seattle hospital. We sat up until
midnight talking about the days of our youth. The
next Monday night, my friend Peris Woodruff left
Earth for a better land.

Juanita wrote a beautiful letter to us. She said that
after the funeral services while the family was gathered in the home, one of the married children refer-
ing to the air controllers' strike then in progress
said: "No old air controller could say to Dad's soul,

'You can't go' and stop its flight straight to God who gave it.' "

A man in the Old Testament called the Preacher reminded us that there is a "time to weep" (Eccl. 3:4).

But . . .

A New Testament preacher spoke from the lonely island of Patmos and said, "God shall wipe away all tears from their eyes; and there shall be no more death, neither sorrow, nor crying, neither shall there be any more pain: for the former things are passed away" (Rev. 21:4).

"Joy to the world! the Lord is come" sang the Christmas card, and the notes were planted in the silicon in the substance of the stars when they sang together as time began.

And the saints will still be singing the song when time shall be no more.

10
Beyond the Sunset

This little book started in the desert. It seems fitting that it end there in the land of its conception.

The daylight miracle was coming to a close. First I noticed the shadows of the Joshua trees. The plateau trail led through the fringes of the largest stand of these shaggy old giants on the earth. And they *were* old, they were giants, some of them forty feet tall. Joshuas are not pretty in the manicured sense, say, of a silver fir with every needle in place and its branches tapering to a starlike point, but they are more interesting. They were named by the early Mormon explorers who were reminded of the Israelite leader who lifted up his arms in prayer before battle in the conquest of Canaan. Each humanlike botanical apparition seemed to be stretching hairy arms in petition to the God who made it. I felt a mystical connection with the whispering convocation as I walked among its reverent members. After all, I thought wryly, God made me too.

As I walked through the strange prayer meeting that afternoon, I remembered that the Joshua is not a tree at all. It is a member of the lily family. My trip into the desert was the week before Easter. I thought of the snow-white Easter lilies that would be gracing church altars in the most sacred day of the year for all Christians throughout the world: Joshua—Jesus. The thought was so compelling that it stopped me in my tracks. Joshua in the Hebrew language means "Jehovah is salvation." This was the message of the angel to Joseph: "Thou shalt call his name Jesus: for he shall save his people from their sins" (Matt. 1:21). I am certain that no such connection was made by the explorers who first named the trees, preoccupied as they were with the Old Testament. I also realize that my analogy is somewhat far stretched, but it lifted my mind and heart.

While I stood in quiet meditation, I noticed something else: The shadows of the trees, lighted by the descending sun, pointed not toward the sunset but toward the east, and the dawning of a new day. The resurrection! The transition from time to eternity—heaven!

Physical darkness was beginning to fall on that part of the earth on which I stood. Another kind of darkness would one day or night fall on me and upon my loved ones and friends. Should any of us who belong to Jesus be afraid of the darkness called death?

The ancient prophet Zechariah spoke beautifully to this question: "It shall be one day which shall be known to the Lord, not day, nor night: but it shall

come to pass, that at evening time it shall be light"
(Zech. 14:7). John reminded us that in heaven there
is no night. The eternal Light is Christ.

Light Without a Shadow

The ancient trees—some of them 1,000 years old
—spoke an ancient message. The shadows began at
their feet and reached in huge, misshapen dark patches toward the morning yet to come. Listen to the
prophet Amos: "Seek him that . . . turneth the shadow of death into the morning" (Amos 5:8).

We do not walk far along life's journey until shadows begin to fall. The older we grow, the more they
seem to multiply.

The Shadow of Disappointed Hopes

We build our castles in the air but never inhabit
them. We sit in the ashes of our burned-out dreams.
Hope fashions a bubble in which a tiny rainbow
flutters, but the bubble bursts with our touching,
and the rainbow vanishes with it. No one of us es-
capes such feelings of frustration.

The Shadows of Heartaches

How often have you heard someone cry, "My
heart is broken"? Friends desert us in our need.
Loved ones fail us. Misunderstandings tear away
our peace of mind. Someone else walks in such a
shadow, and we walk vicariously in that shadow too.

The Shadows of Sin

Burning conscience sears, and guilt rides upon us. This is our inheritance from Eden. We finally find relief through Christ our Lord and Savior and the knowledge that there is no sin in heaven. Yet the shadows come back. As long as we are in these physical bodies, we shall know sin. We shall sin but not through the choice of spirit. When we do so, we shall also walk awhile in shadow. That is because we know that we have hurt the heart of God.

The Shadows of Pain

How these mortal bodies suffer! It is one of the costs of being alive in the flesh. For some, death comes as the only relief they can find for endless suffering. Even harder for us to bear is the suffering of the one we love more than anyone else on earth.

The Shadow of Death

Ah, but the psalmist, touched by a coal from the altar of God, cried out in exultation, "Yea, though I walk through the . . . shadow of death, . . . thou art with me; . . . I will dwell in the house of the Lord for ever" (Ps. 23:4-6); that last great shadow is lifted!

There are no such shadows in heaven as those we have known on earth. In that great, glad morning when the heavens have been dissolved—the sun, the moon, the stars have melted away—when time has been lost in eternity, we shall enter into the city foursquare. John saw the glorious vision from Patmos: "The city had no need of the sun, neither of the moon, to shine in it: for the glory of God did lighten it, and the Lamb is the light thereof" (Rev. 21:23).

Joy Forever

Ask any Christian, What do you want most in heaven? If your experience parallels my own, the answer will be: "I want most to see my Lord face-to-face, to thank Him for what He has done for me. Then I want to see my loved ones again." It is nearly always so. But the Bible leaves so many questions unanswered. Perhaps it is because our finite minds could never understand the infinite answers.

I once said, more or less jokingly, to my friend, Dr. James Sullivan, former president of the Baptist Sunday School Board, "I don't think I want to go to heaven." He asked, "Why not?" I said, "Because the Bible says just one thing about what we'll do there. It says that we'll all dress up in white robes, gather around the throne, and sing the song of Moses and the Lamb, and I don't even know the tune."

Sullivan laughed heartily. Then he said, "Well, I am sure, Harold, the Lord will find something for you to do."

I have never found happiness on earth without my being busy. I doubt that you have either. It is God's own nature to work, and He imparted that nature to us. We need to rest—but not all the time. We shudder at the thought of spending ten trillion times ten trillion years—or what passes for years—doing nothing at all.

Of course, the Bible says much about rest. In one of the sweetest invitations ever given, Jesus said, "Come unto me, all ye that labour and are heavy laden, and I will give you rest" (Matt. 11:28). There is also rest from our labors in heaven: "I heard a voice from heaven saying unto me, Write, Blessed are the dead which die in the Lord from henceforth: Yea, saith the Spirit, that they may rest from their labours; and their works do follow them" (Rev. 14:13).

But we need more. We do not know what our glorified bodies will be like. We do know that we shall know each other even as we are known. We know each other on earth more by our character than by our looks, by our influence more than by our presence.

Let me tell you about Mrs. Willie. I went to see her and learned more about heaven. She lay in bed with her delicate body propped up by pillows. The light from a tilting bed lamp splashed over the open book on the coverlet, and her fingers were tracing with a fountain pen the answers to a series of questions. She looked up at me with a smile and replaced the cap on her fountain pen. She stretched out a thin hand to me. With the movement, the little blue volume on the bed closed. I was startled by the title looking up at me, *Guiding the Junior Boys and Girls in the Sunday School.*

I was making my periodic call. I liked to come to

see Mrs. Willie. I had been calling on her for more than ten years. That was when I first learned that she and her small family had moved to town but that she was bedfast with tuberculosis. I had gone then to bring her a portion of comfort and strength as any pastor would.

But I was the one who received the strength.

I found myself in the presence of one of the most vital personalities I ever met. She was not complaining at her fate. She was not even worried. With a gracious smile, she acknowledged my presence and weakly gripped my hand in hers. Before I left, she asked me to read the fourteenth chapter of John. Then we prayed together. After that, it was easy for me to go back. In fact, I just had to. I needed for myself something of the same faith she had.

Now, after ten years, I was still calling on the little woman who was still bedfast. According to the doctors, she would never rise from that bed to live as other women did. This flashed through my mind after my first startled recognition of the title of the little book on her bed. Did she know what the doctors were saying?

"I see that you are busy at work," I said, obviously.

"I am always at work," she answered. "There is so much to do and so little time to do it."

My throat suddenly choked up. After a moment I reached over and took the study course book from the bedclothes. Idly, I turned the pages. Here and there outstanding statements were underscored in ink.

"I see you are getting ready to teach a class in our Sunday school," I said, and I could have bitten my tongue out.

Mrs. Willie laughed. It was a low, rippling, pleasent sound.

"You are surprised to find me studying this book," she challenged. "It sticks out all over you. Now, just why should you be surprised?"

I was speechless. How could I tell her that she would probably never get well enough to teach a Sunday School class, that she was wasting her time on something that would never do her any good? I was so thoroughly miserable that I could not meet her smiling eyes.

"All right, then, I'll tell you. You know that the doctors have given up my case as hopeless. You know also that I am aware of that. You think that there is not the slightest chance of my ever putting to use what I am learning in this little book. But you are making a mistake. I shall put it to use."

I forced myself to look at her face, but she was looking out of the window at the far outlines of the Organ Mountains to the east, and her voice was whispery and throbbing with deep emotion. There were no tears. I leaned forward so I would not miss a single word.

"It won't be long," said my friend, "before I shall leave this earthly tabernacle—it has not served me too well, after all—and I shall go to that one which

God will fashion for me eternal in the heavens. And when I get there, I shall not ask for a thousand years in which to rest. Oh, no! I shall fall at the feet of my dear Savior and say, 'Please, dear Lord, give me another Junior Bible school class. I want to keep telling the old, old story.' " She paused a moment. "That's why I am studying now."

The room seemed full of angels.

When I get to heaven, I expect to see Mrs. Willie surrounded by boys and girls. She will be telling them about the love of Christ.

Finis

When Earth's last picture is painted and the tubes
    are twisted and dried,
When the oldest colours have faded, and the young-
    est critic has died,
We shall rest, and, faith, we shall need it—lie down
    for an aeon or two,
Till the Master of All Good Workmen shall set us to
    work anew.
And those that were good shall be happy: they shall
    sit in a golden chair;
They shall splash at a ten-league canvas with
    brushes of comets' hair.
They shall find real saints to draw from—Magda-
    lene, Peter, and Paul;
They shall work an age at a sitting and never grow
    tired at all!
And only The Master shall praise us, and only The
    Master shall blame;
And no one shall work for money, and no one shall
    work for fame,

But each for the joy of working, and each, in his
    separate star,
Shall draw the Thing as he sees It for the God of
    Things as They are!

—Kipling